SEASIDE HOTELS

edited by Martin Nicholas Kunz

teNeues

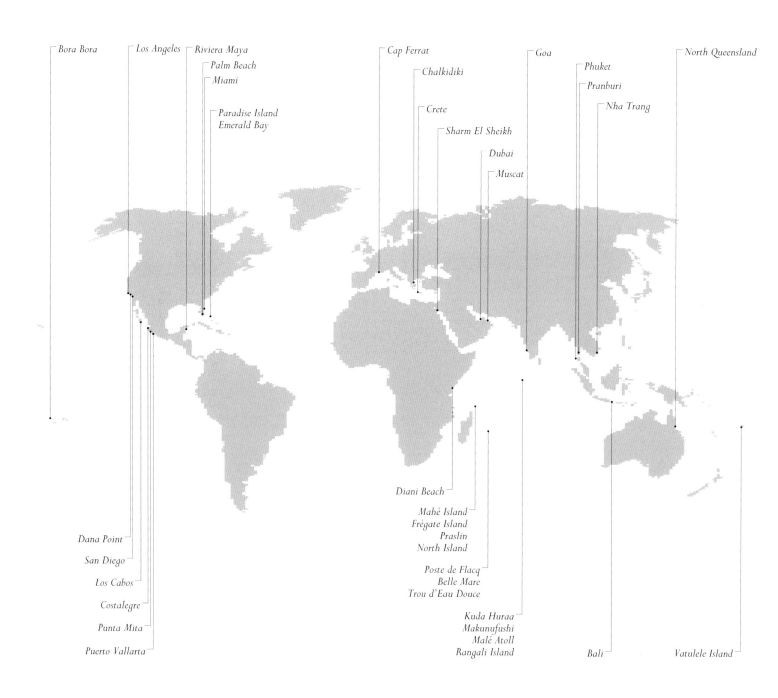

Bora Bora

Los Angeles

Riviera Maya

Palm Beach

Miami

Paradise Island
Emerald Bay

Cap Ferrat

Chalkidiki

Crete

Sharm El Sheikh

Dubai

Muscat

Goa

Phuket

Pranburi

Nha Trang

North Queensland

Dana Point

San Diego

Los Cabos

Costalegre

Punta Mita

Puerto Vallarta

Diani Beach

Mahé Island
Frégate Island
Praslin
North Island

Poste de Flacq
Belle Mare
Trou d'Eau Douce

Kuda Huraa
Makunufushi
Malé Atoll
Rangali Island

Bali

Vatulele Island

Seaside Hotels

Luxury is a question of time

Today everything appears to be luxury. In every area of life, it seems to meet us; waits for us everywhere. The term was so overused in recent years, even misused, that it has lost a bit of its shine. Every host not waiting with exactly cheap prices declares their product or service to be "luxury". Those who can offer genuine exclusivity have a hard time placed against all the pseudo-luxury. An absurd "arms race" arises in the terminology that forces one host to try to overtrump the others with new word creations.

The beach hotels presented in this book can be easily classified into the category "Extra Premium" (a word creation from marketing expert Tyler Brulé); they are waiting with something really extraordinary. Their special luxury: exclusive access to the ocean and dreamy sand beaches. In times of mass tourism, it is anything but easy to find a quiet place to bathe. But, on the "private beach" of a hotel the guest occasionally has the water to itself, at least the beaches are never overcrowded and the bathers are not herded together on a few square meters, towel to towel. On the contrary: many hotels have kilometer-long beaches or an own inlet, for instance the Seychelles resort of North Island or Frégate Private Island, where there are even more beaches than guests. In some hotel facilities, the individual buildings are placed at great distance from each other in the woods, so one can feel like Robinson on a lonely island. That offers complete quiet and seclusion—a luxury in hectic times.

But the exclusivity of a first-class hotel is best reflected in other things, for example in the furnishings: baths completely made from marble are now almost obligatory. Each hotel also offers an additional specialty. At one, the guest can bathe in a heated saltwater pool, at another, in a plunge pool cut from lava, in which seawater is mixed with fresh spring water. One can sleep pleasantly in a four-posted bed made of mahogany, and in one hotel built right on the ocean, the guests can look into the water through a glass floor. And what is the difference in the service of a luxury lodge compared with the standard? For example, some hotels have employed their own butlers who individually take care of each guest in a suite.

Is that all really necessary? This question is asked quickly and one gets involved in an envy-discussion, whether or not it is unjust that only a small part of society can afford the mentioned exclusivity. But it is often the positive effects that luxury can generally offer that are overlooked. To produce it requires creativity, it always brings forth something special from a culture and from technology. For instance, the ceiling and wall murals or the applied arts in old castles would never have developed to full bloom without the luxury demands of the aristocracy. And today, the joy of the financially sound also lets something new emerge. Luxury creates progress. Especially in the area of technology: if the automobile used to be reserved for a rich minority, nowadays almost everyone utilizes it, likewise televisions, stereo systems, or cell phones. All this demonstrates: luxury is a question of time. Those sitting at the crest and creating something exclusive will always find copycats who want to have the benefit of luxury and who may just be able to create it with less expenditure. So far until it has finally become affordable, lost its exclusivity, and is accessible to the wide masses. The envy-discussion is invalid at that point, because that which was once luxury has contributed to lifting the general standard of living. Luxury is largely transient; it is usually just a matter of time. The luxury of today will become the standard of tomorrow.

This probably also applies to the hotels that can be viewed on the following pages. Some things, presented here as luxurious, currently avant-garde and perhaps even appearing a bit decadent, might be found in hotels that are not so exclusive in ten, twenty or thirty years hence. Let's look forward to that!

Christian Schönwetter

Luxus ist eine Frage der Zeit

Heute scheint alles Luxus zu sein. In jedem Bereich des Lebens scheint er uns entgegenzuwinken, überall wartet er angeblich auf uns. Der Begriff wurde in den letzten Jahren so inflationär verwendet, ja geradezu missbraucht, dass er sich ein wenig abgenutzt hat. Jeder Anbieter, der nicht gerade Billigpreise offeriert, deklariert sein Produkt oder seine Dienstleistung als „Luxus". Wer dagegen mit wirklicher Exklusivität aufwarten kann, hat es schwer sich gegen all den Pseudoluxus abzusetzen. Es entsteht ein absurdes „Wettrüsten" bei den Begriffen, das die Anbieter dazu zwingt, sich mit immer neuen Wortschöpfungen gegenseitig zu übertrumpfen.

Die Strandhotels, die in diesem Buch vorgestellt werden, ließen sich ohne weiteres in die Kategorie „Über-Premium" (eine Wortschöpfung des Marken-Experten Tyler Brulé) einordnen, sie warten mit wirklich Außerordentlichem auf. Ihr spezieller Luxus: Exklusiver Zugang zum Meer und traumhafter Sandstrand. In Zeiten des Massentourismus ist es alles andere als einfach, stille Orte zum Baden zu finden. Am „Privatstrand" eines Hotels jedoch hat der Gast das Wasser mitunter ganz für sich allein, zumindest sind die Liegeflächen niemals überfüllt und die Badenden nicht Handtuch an Handtuch auf wenigen Quadratmetern zusammengepfercht. Im Gegenteil: Viele Häuser verfügen über kilometerlange Strände oder eigene Buchten wie zum Beispiel die Seychellen Resorts North Island oder Frégate Private Island, wo es selbst bei voller Belegung mehr Strände als Gäste gibt. Bei einigen Hotelanlagen sind die Einzelgebäude mit großem Abstand zueinander im Wald platziert, so dass man sich wie Robinson auf einer einsamen Insel fühlen darf. Sie bieten völlige Ruhe und Abgeschiedenheit – auch ein Luxus in einer hektischen Zeit.

Doch die Exklusivität eines Spitzenhotels schlägt sich auch in anderen Dingen nieder, etwa in der Ausstattung: Bäder ganz aus Marmor gehören inzwischen beinahe schon zum Pflichtprogramm. Jedes Haus wartet zusätzlich mit einer anderen Besonderheit auf. Einmal kann der Gast in einem beheizten Salzwasserpool baden, ein anderes Mal in einem in Lavastein gehauenen Tauchbecken, in dem Meerwasser mit frischem Quellwasser vermischt wird. In Himmelbetten aus Mahagoni lässt es sich angenehm schlafen, und bei einem direkt ins Meer gebauten Hotel können die Gäste durch einen Glasboden ins Wasser schauen. Und wie unterscheidet sich der Service einer Luxusherberge von dem einer gewöhnlichen? Zum Beispiel haben einige Häuser eigene Butler engagiert, die sich ganz individuell nur um die Gäste je einer Suite kümmern.

Ist das alles wirklich nötig? Diese Frage wird schnell gestellt, und sofort gerät man in eine Neid-Diskussion darüber, ob es nicht ungerecht sei, dass sich nur ein kleiner Teil der Gesellschaft Exklusivitäten der genannten Art leisten kann. Doch häufig werden die positiven Auswirkungen, die Luxus ganz allgemein haben kann, übersehen. Ihn zu erzeugen, erfordert Kreativität, er bringt immer wieder kulturell wie technisch Außerordentliches hervor. So hätten sich etwa die Decken- und Wandmalerei oder das Kunsthandwerk in alten Schlössern ohne das Luxusbedürfnis der Aristokratie nie zur vollen Blüte entwickeln können. Und auch heute ist es so, dass die Freude der Zahlungskräftigen an Besonderem auch Neues entstehen lässt. Luxus schafft Fortschritt. Vor allem im Bereich der Technik: War etwa das Auto früher einer reichen Minderheit vorbehalten, benutzt es heute fast jedermann, ebenso das Fernsehgerät, die Stereo-Anlage oder das Mobiltelefon. All dies zeigt: Luxus ist eine Frage der Zeit. Wer sich an die Spitze setzt und etwas besonders Exklusives schafft, findet immer Nachahmer, die in den Genuss des gleichen Luxus kommen möchten, und denen es vielleicht gelingt, ihn mit geringerem Aufwand zu erzeugen. So lange, bis er schließlich so erschwinglich geworden ist, dass er seine Exklusivität verliert und auch für die breite Masse zugänglich wird. In diesem Moment ist die Neid-Diskussion hinfällig, denn nun hat der Luxus von einst dazu beigetragen, den allgemeinen Lebensstandard ein wenig zu heben. Luxus ist also in hohem Maße vergänglich, ist meist nur eine Sache auf Zeit. Der Luxus von heute wird zum Standard von morgen.

Dies gilt wahrscheinlich auch für die Hotels, die auf den folgenden Seiten zu sehen sind. Einiges, was hier als luxuriös vorgestellt wird, was heute avantgardistisch und vielleicht sogar ein wenig dekadent anmuten mag, wird möglicherweise in zehn, zwanzig oder dreißig Jahren auch in nicht ganz so exklusiven Hotels zu finden sein. Freuen wir uns schon jetzt darauf!

Christian Schönwetter

Le luxe est une question de temps

Aujourd'hui, tout semble être luxurieux. Dans tous les domaines de la vie, il semble nous faire des clins d'œil et il semble nous attendre partout. Ce terme a été utilisé de façon tellement excessive, oui même à tort et à travers, qu'il a perdu de son sens. Chaque fournisseur, pour peu qu'il ne propose pas des prix bon marché, déclare que son produit ou son service est luxurieux. Celui, cependant, qui peut offrir un réel raffinement, a du mal à se distinguer par rapport à tous ces pseudos luxes. C'est une véritable « course aux mots » totalement absurde qui se met en place et qui force les fournisseurs à renchérir sans cesse par de nouvelles créations langagières.

Les hôtels de bord de mer, présentés dans ce livre, appartiennent sans contexte à la catégorie « premium supérieur » (une création langagière de l'expert en marques Tyler Brulé) ; ils offrent vraiment des choses l'extraordinaires. Leur luxe particulier : un accès exclusif à la mer et une plage d'un sable de rêve. A l'époque du tourisme de masse, il est tout sauf facile de trouver des lieux tranquilles où se baigner. Sur la « plage privée » d'un hôtel, l'hôte peut jouir de l'eau tout seul ; tout du moins, les plages ne sont jamais surchargées et les baigneurs jamais les uns sur les autres comme parqués sur quelques mètres carrés. Tout au contraire : de nombreuses maisons disposent de plages immenses, s'étendant sur des kilomètres, ou de baies privées comme, par exemple, le Seychellen Resorts North Island ou le Frégate Private Island, où même lorsque l'hôtel est complet, le nombre de plage dépassera toujours celui des clients. Dans certains établissements, les bâtiments individuels sont si espacés dans la forêt les uns des autres que l'on a l'impression d'être Robinson sur son île déserte. Ils offrent un calme et un isolement total — un vrai luxe à notre époque frénétique.

Mais cependant, le raffinement d'un hôtel de haut niveau est visible dans d'autres domaines, comme dans l'aménagement : les salles de bains complètement en marbre font presque partie maintenant de l'offre standard. Mais chaque maison offre quelque chose de bien particulier, en supplément. Ici, l'hôte peut se baigner dans une piscine chauffée d'eau salée, là, dans un bassin de pierres de lave dans lequel l'eau de mer est mélangée à de l'eau fraîche de source. C'est un plaisir de dormir dans un lit à baldaquin en acajou, et, dans un hôtel construit sur la mer, les hôtes peuvent regarder directement dans l'eau au-travers d'un sol de verre. Et qu'est-ce qui distingue les services offerts dans un établissement de luxe à ceux d'un établissement habituel ? Certaines maisons ont, par exemple, engagé des serviteurs chargés de s'occuper exclusivement des hôtes d'une suite donnée.

Mais, tout cela est-il vraiment indispensable ? Il est facile de poser cette question, mais on retombe rapidement dans une discussion nourrie de jalousie qui consiste à savoir s'il n'est pas injuste que seule une petite partie de la société puisse se payer de tels raffinements. Cependant, bien souvent, on omet de considérer les effets positifs généraux que le luxe a. Le produire demande de la créativité ; il génère toujours de l'extraordinaire que ce soit au niveau culturel que technique. Ainsi, les fresques et les plafonds ou l'artisanats d'art des vieux châteaux n'auraient jamais pu voir le jour si l'aristocratie n'avait pas ressenti le désir de posséder du luxe. Il en est exactement de même aujourd'hui : le plaisir des plus riches à goûter du particulier génère de la nouveauté. Le luxe entraîne le progrès. Surtout dans le domaine de la technique : l'automobile autrefois l'apanage d'une minorité, est utilisée aujourd'hui par chacun, de même pour la télévision, la chaîne stéréo ou le téléphone portable. Tout cela prouve que le luxe est une question de temps. Celui qui se place à la pointe du progrès et crée quelque chose d'exclusif, trouvera toujours des copieurs, qui désireront jouir du même luxe ; ceux-ci trouveront peut-être une solution d'y arriver avec un moindre effort ; jusqu'à ce que cela devienne si bon marché que ça perdra son exclusivité et deviendra accessible à tous. C'est bien là où la discussion nourrie de jalousie perd sa pertinence, puisque le luxe d'autrefois a permis d'élever un peu le niveau de vie général. Le luxe est donc éminemment fugace, limité, le plus souvent, dans le temps. Le luxe d'aujourd'hui deviendra le standard de demain.

Ceci est vraisemblablement aussi valable pour les hôtels présentés dans les pages suivantes. Certaines des choses présentées ici comme étant luxurieuses, ce qui aujourd'hui appartient à l'avant-garde et peut être même considéré comme étant un peu décadent, sera peut-être aussi offert dans dix, vingt ou trente ans dans des hôtels moins raffinés. Réjouissons-nous à l'avance !

Christian Schönwetter

Lujo es una cuestión de tiempo

Hoy en día todo parece ser lujo. Parece saludarnos en cada ámbito de la vida, supuestamente en todas partes nos espera. En los últimos años el concepto lujo se ha usado excesivamente, se ha abusado de él, reduciéndolo a un término que ahora suena algo desgastado. Todo aquel que ofrece un producto o un servicio dice que éstos son de lujo, a no ser que sea un ofertante de precios baratos especiales. Quien realmente puede ofrecer la exclusividad tiene dificultades para distinguirse de tanto seudo-lujo. Lo que resulta es una absurda "carrera de armamento" conceptual que obliga a todos a superarse mutuamente con creaciones de palabras cada vez más novedosas.

Los hoteles de playa que se presentan en este volumen se pueden clasificar sin duda alguna en la categoría "Über Premium" (un término creado por el experto de marcas Tyler Brulé). Todos son verdaderamente extraordinarios. Su lujo excepcional: El acceso exclusivo al mar y a una playa de ensueño. En esta época de turismo de masas no es nada fácil encontrar un lugar tranquilo para bañarse. Pero en la "playa privada" de un hotel el huésped tiene de vez en cuando el mar sólo para él; al menos siempre hay espacio libre para tumbarse y los bañistas no tienen que estar apiñados uno al lado del otro en unos pocos metros cuadrados. Por el contrario: Muchos hoteles disponen de kilómetros de playa o de bahías propias, como por ejemplo los resorts North Island o Frégate Private Island en las islas Seychelles, donde, incluso estando llenos, hay más playas que huéspedes. En algunos de los hoteles las construcciones se encuentran en medio de la vegetación a bastante distancia unas de otras, de tal manera que uno puede sentirse como Robinson en una isla solitaria. Ofrecen una paz absoluta y total aislamiento –también un lujo en el agitado mundo de hoy.

Pero la exclusividad de un hotel de primera se refleja también en otros elementos. Por ejemplo, en el mobiliario y la decoración: Los baños completamente de mármol son ya casi una obligación. Cada establecimiento presenta adicionalmente algún detalle especial. En uno, es la posibilidad de bañarse en una piscina de agua de mar climatizada, en otro, en una piscina esculpida en piedra de lava en la que se han mezclado agua de mar y agua de manantial. Camas de caoba con dosel para dormir agradablemente y un hotel construido directamente sobre el mar, donde los huéspedes pueden mirar el agua a través de suelos de cristal. ¿Y en que se diferencia el servicio de un hotel de lujo con el de uno común y corriente? Algunos hoteles, por ejemplo, han contratado sus propios mayordomos que se ocupan de forma individual y exclusiva de los huéspedes de cada suite.

¿Es todo esto realmente necesario? Esa pregunta se hace muy rápido e inmediatamente se cae en la trampa de la envidia y se discute sobre si es justo o no que sólo una mínima parte de la sociedad pueda permitirse el exclusivo lujo antes mencionado. Pero a menudo se dejan de lado los efectos positivos que el lujo en general puede tener. Crear lujo requiere creatividad y al mismo tiempo se generan una y otra vez excepcionales avances técnicos y culturales. Los frescos y los murales, o la artesanía, de los antiguos castillos, nunca hubieran alcanzado su pleno esplendor sin el ansia de lujo de la aristocracia. Y también hoy el gusto que encuentran las personas ricas en lo especial produce novedades. El lujo genera progreso. Sobre todo en el área de la técnica: Si antiguamente los coches estaban reservados para una minoría rica, hoy los utiliza casi todo el mundo; igual sucede con la televisión, los equipos de música o el teléfono móvil. Todo esto demuestra que: Lujo es una cuestión de tiempo. Aquel que está a la vanguardia y crea algo exclusivo, encuentra siempre imitadores, que quieren disfrutar del mismo lujo, y tal vez logren crearlo con menos recursos. Hasta que finalmente sea tan asequible, que pierda toda su exclusividad y esté al alcance de una inmensa mayoría. En ese momento ya no habrá lugar para envidias y discusiones, pues el lujo de entonces habrá contribuido a elevar un poco el nivel de vida general. Así pues, el lujo es pasajero, es casi siempre una cuestión de tiempo. El lujo de hoy es el estándar de mañana.

Esto probablemente también sea válido para los hoteles que se presentan a continuación. Algunos de los elementos que aquí se muestran como lujosos y vanguardistas, y que incluso pueden parecer algo decadentes, probablemente en diez, veinte o treinta años se encontrarán también en hoteles no tan exclusivos. Alegrémonos ya de que así sea!

Christian Schönwetter

Il lusso è una questione di tempo

Oggi tutto sembra essere di lusso. In ogni settore della vita sembra salutarci, apparentemente ci sta aspettando ovunque. Il termine in questi ultimi anni è stato utilizzato in modo così inflazionale, quasi abusato che oggi si presenta un poco logorato. Ogni offerente – che non sia proprio un offerente di prezzi stracciati – dichiara il suo prodotto o il suo servizio come "lusso". Chi invece è in grado di presentare la vera esclusività, fa fatica a distinguersi da tutto questo pseudolusso. Ne nasce una gara per l'uso dei termini che obbliga tutti gli offerenti di superarsi a vicenda con sempre più nuove creazioni di termini.

I beach hotel presentati in questo volume potrebbero senz'altro essere inseriti nella categoria del "Supremo" (un termine creato dall'esperto di marche Tyler Brulé), si presentano con vera straordinarietà. Il loro lusso speciale: accesso esclusivo al mare e spiagge di sabbia da sogno. Ai tempi del turismo di massa non è affatto facile trovare luoghi tranquilli per fare il bagno. Su una "spiaggia privata" di un hotel invece l'ospite a volte ha a disposizione l'acqua tutta per sé, almeno le aree per prendere il sole non sono mai affollate ed i bagnanti non si trovano telo contro telo schiacciati su pochi metri quadri. Al contrario:molte case dispongono di spiagge lunghe dei chilometri o baie private come ad esempio i resorts North Island o Frégate Island sulle isole Seychelles ove anche in caso dell'hotel completo esistono comunque più spiagge che clienti. In alcuni impianti degli hotel i singoli edifici sono posizionati a grande distanza tra di loro in mezzo ad un bosco in modo che ci si può sentire come Robinson sull'isola deserta. Offrono assoluta tranquillità e solitudine – anche questo è un lusso ai tempi stressanti d'oggi.

Ma l'esclusività di un hotel di lusso si vede anche in altre cose come ad esempio nell'arredamento. Stanze da bagno tutte di marmo oggigiorno fanno quasi parte dello standard. Ogni casa presenta inoltre una sua particolarità. Una volta l'ospite può fare il bagno in una piscina d'acqua di mare riscaldata, un'altra volta in una vasca d'immersione fatta di pietra vulcanica ove l'acqua di mare è mescolata all'acqua fresca di fonte. Ci si dorme bene nei letti a baldacchino fatti di mogano ed in un hotel costruito direttamente sul mare, gli ospiti possono osservare l'acqua attraverso un pavimento di vetro. E come si distingue il servizio di un albergo di lusso da uno normale? Ad esempio alcuni hotel hanno impiegato dei serventi che si occupano di ogni ospite di una suite individualmente.

Tutto ciò è veramente necessario? Questa domanda è fatta velocemente e subito ci si entra in una discussione dettata dall'invidia, se non è ingiusto che soltanto una piccola parte della società si possa permettere le esclusività di questo genere. Ma spesso si tralascia di vedere gli effetti positivi del lusso in genere. Convincerlo richiede creatività, e produce sempre di nuovo lo straordinario, sia a livello culturale che tecnico. Ad esempio le decorazioni di pareti e soffitti o l'artigianato artistico nei vecchi castelli non si sarebbero mai potuto sviluppare a tale perfezione se non ci fosse stato l'esigenza di lusso dell'aristocrazia. Anche oggi la gioia di chi è solvente di avere cose particolari fa nascere del nuovo. Lusso crea progresso. Soprattutto nella tecnica. Se la macchina ai tempi vecchi era riservata ad una ricca minorità, oggi la usa quasi ognuno, così come la tv, lo stereo, il telefonino. Tutto ciò fa vedere: lusso è una questione di tempo. Chi si mette in cima creando qualcosa di esclusivo troverà sempre imitatori che vogliono godersi lo stesso lusso ed i quali forse riescono a crearlo con meno dispendio. Fino al momento in cui è diventato così accessibile che perde la sua esclusività diventando accessibile per la massa. In questo momento la discussione d'invidia decade perché ora il lusso di una volta ha contribuito ad alzare un poco lo standard di vita. Il lusso è quindi altamente effimero, molte volte è soltanto una questione di tempo. Il lusso d'oggi diventa lo standard di domani.

Ciò vale probabilmente anche per gli hotel presentati sulle seguenti pagine. Quello che è presentato qui come di lusso, quello che oggi può sembrare all'avanguardia e forse addirittura un poco decadente, magari tra dieci, venti o trenta anni si troverà anche negli alberghi meno esclusivi. Rallegriamoci già da adesso!

Christian Schönwetter

Hotel del Coronado
San Diego, California

A house with a glorious past: It was erected in 1888 in the Victorian style, in 1958 Billy Wilder at this location made the film "Some like it hot" and in 1977 it was finally declared to be a historic monument. The list of guest reads like a Who's Who of the United States: the actors Charlie Chaplin and Brad Pitt, the writers Tennessee Williams and Arthur Miller, the singers Barbra Streisand and Madonna, the presidents Franklin Roosevelt and Ronald Reagan—all these people have visited the hotel.

Ein Haus mit glorreicher Vergangenheit: 1888 wurde es im viktorianischen Stil errichtet, 1958 drehte Billy Wilder hier den Film „Manche mögen's heiß" und 1977 wurde es schließlich zum Denkmal erklärt. Die Gästeliste des Hotels liest sich wie ein Who's Who der Vereinigten Staaten: die Schauspieler Charlie Chaplin und Brad Pitt, die Schriftsteller Tennessee Williams und Arthur Miller, die Sängerinnen Barbra Streisand und Madonna, die Präsidenten Franklin Roosevelt und Ronald Reagan – sie alle haben das Hotel besucht.

Une maison au passé illustre : Elle fut érigée en 1888 dans le style victorien, en 1958, Billy Wilder y tournait le film « Certains l'aiment chaud » et elle fut enfin classée en 1977 comme monument historique. La lecture de la liste des clients de l'hôtel rappelle celle du Who's Who des Etats-Unis : les acteurs Charlie Chaplin et Brad Pitt, les écrivains Tennessee Williams et Arthur Miller, les chanteurs Barbra Streisand et Madonna, les présidents Franklin Roosevelt et Ronald Reagan – tous ont visités cet hôtel.

Una casa con un pasado glorioso: Fue construida en 1888 en estilo victoriano, en 1958 Billy Wilder la usó como escenario para la película "Con faldas y a lo loco" y en 1977 fue declarada patrimonio nacional. La lista de huéspedes del hotel parece una lista de personalidades de los Estados Unidos: Los actores Charlie Chaplin y Brad Pitt, los escritores Tennessee Williams y Arthur Miller, las cantantes Barbra Streisand y Madonna, los presidentes Franklin Roosevelt y Ronald Reagan –todos han visitado este hotel.

Una casa con un passato glorioso: Nel 1888 è stato eretto nello stile vittoriano, nel 1958 Billy Wilder qui ha girato il film "A qualcuno piace caldo" e nel 1977 finalmente è stato dichiarato monumento storico. La lista degli ospiti dell'hotel si legge come il Who's Who degli Stati Uniti: Gli attori Charlie Chaplin e Brad Pitt, gli scrittori Tennessee Williams ed Arthur Miller, le cantanti Barbra Streisand e Madonna, i Presidenti Franklin Roosevelt e Ronald Reagan – loro tutti hanno visitato l'hotel.

The sweeping property is surrounded on all sides by palm trees.
Das weitläufige Anwesen ist an allen Seiten von Palmen umstellt.
Cet immense domaine est entouré de toutes parts de palmiers.
El amplio recinto está completamente rodeado de palmeras.
La vasta tenuta è circondata da tutte le parti da palme.

The interior *tells about the century old history of the hotel.*

Die Einrichtung *erzählt von der über hundertjährigen Geschichte des Hotels.*

L'aménagement *rappelle l'histoire de l'hôtel longue de plus de cent ans.*

La decoración *del hotel da testimonio de su historia de más de un siglo.*

L'arredamento *racconta la storia oltre centenaria dell'hotel.*

Shutters on the Beach
Los Angeles, California

The lamella shutters, responsible for the name, are characteristic for the only genuine beach hotel in Los Angeles. Its architecture revives the tradition of the great Californian beach hotels of the 20's. The 186 guestrooms are largely kept white, each enjoys the luxury of a marble bath with a whirlpool tub, most have a view of the beach and the Santa Monica pier.

Kennzeichnend für das einzige echte Beach Hotel in Los Angeles sind die Lamellen-Läden, die dem Haus den Namen geben. Seine Architektur lässt die Tradition der großen kalifornischen Strandhotels aus den 20er Jahren wieder aufleben. Die 186 Gästezimmer sind größtenteils in Weiß gehalten, jedes genießt den Luxus eines Marmorbads mit Whirlpool-Wanne, die meisten haben eine Aussicht auf den Strand und den Pier von Santa Monica.

La particularité du seul vrai hôtel en bord de mer de Los Angeles sont ses volets en lamelles qui donnent son nom à la maison. Son architecture fait revivre la tradition des grands hôtels en bordure de mer des années 20. Les 186 chambres d'hôtes sont pour la plupart en blanc, chaque chambre arbore le luxe d'une salle de bains en marbre dotée d'une baignoire-jacuzzi, la plupart donnent sur la plage et la jetée de Santa Monica.

Elemento característico del único auténtico hotel de playa de Los Angeles son los postigos de listones que le dan su nombre. Su arquitectura revive la tradición de los grandes hoteles de playa californianos de los años 20. Las 186 habitaciones son en su gran mayoría blancas, todas ofrecen el lujo de un baño de mármol con jacuzzi, la mayoría tiene vista de la playa y del muelle de Santa Monica.

L'unico vero beach hotel a Los Angeles è caratterizzato dalle sue persiane che danno il nome all'hotel. La sua architettura lascia rivivere la tradizione dei grandi beach hotel degli anni 20. Le 186 camere sono maggiormente tenute in colore bianco, ognuna delle quali gode del lusso di una vasca ad idromassaggio, inoltre la maggior parte dispone della vista sulla spiaggia e sul molo di Santa Monica.

One can purvey the Pacific from the pool.

Vom Pool aus kann der Blick über den Pazifik schweifen.

Depuis la piscine, il est possible de caresser du regard le Pacifique.

Desde la piscina se disfruta de la vista del Pacífico.

Dalla piscina lo sguardo può vagare sul Pacifico.

Chairs and tables made of dark warm wood stand in contrast to the otherwise homogenous bright coloration.

Stühle und Tische aus dunklem, warmem Holz stehen im Kontrast zur sonst homogen hellen Farbgebung.

Les chaises et les tables sont construites dans un bois de couleur sombre et chaude et contrastent avec la clarté homogène du reste de la pièce.

Las sillas y las mesas de madera oscura hacen contraste con el claro colorido homogéneo predominante.

Sedie e tavoli fatti di un legno scuro e caldo formano il contrasto alla rimanente colorazione omogeneamente chiara.

The color white dominates the rooms and emits a neutral background for the ocean's dynamic lighting atmospheres.

Die Farbe Weiß dominiert in den Zimmern und gibt einen neutralen Hintergrund für die wechselnden Lichtstimmungen des Meeres ab.

La couleur blanche domine dans les chambres et offre un fond neutre aux jeux de lumière de la mer.

El color blanco predomina en las habitaciones y proporciona un fondo neutral para los colores cambiantes del mar.

Nelle camere domina il colore bianco dando così un sottofondo neutro per captare le luci alternanti del mare.

St. Regis Monarch Beach Resort & Spa

Dana Point, California

So to say, this hotel relocates Italy from the Mediterranean to the Pacific Ocean. The buildings are built Tuscan style so the guest can feel as if on an Italian piazza. A golf course tempts one to sporting activities while in the spa water platters down a three-storey wall and sends forth a gentle background during massages and other wellness applications. The ballroom is especially magnificent with its coffered ceiling, frescos, and alabaster chandeliers.

Dieses Hotel verlegt sozusagen Italien vom Mittelmeer an den Pazifischen Ozean. Die Bauten sind im Toskana-Stil errichtet, sodass der Gast sich wie auf einer italienischen Piazza fühlen kann. Ein Golfplatz lädt zu sportlicher Betätigung ein, während im Spa Wasser eine drei Stockwerke hohe Wand hinabplätschert und eine sanfte Geräuschkulisse bei Massagen und anderen Wellness-Anwendungen abgibt. Besonders prunkvoll ist der Ballsaal mit Kassettendecke, Fresken und Alabaster-Kronleuchtern.

Cet hôtel transpose, pour ainsi dire, l'Italie de la mer Méditerranée à l'Océan Pacifique. Les bâtiments ont été construits dans le style de la Toscane, si bien que l'hôte a l'impression de se trouver sur une piazza italienne. Un golf invite à faire du sport, pendant que dans le domaine spa l'eau dégringole en cascade d'une hauteur de trois étages et offre un doux décor sonore aux massages et aux autres offres de bien-être. La salle de balle est particulièrement somptueuse avec son plafond à caissons, ses fresques et ses lustres en albâtre.

Este hotel traslada, por así decirlo, la Italia mediterránea al Océano Pacífico. El complejo está diseñado en estilo Toscana, de tal forma que el huésped se puede sentir como en una piazza italiana. Un campo de golf invita a la actividad deportiva, mientras que en el Spa rueda el agua por una inmensa pared de tres pisos de altura proporcionando un murmullo suave como ambiente sonoro para los masajes y otras actividades de wellness. Especialmente suntuoso es el salón de baile con sus artesonados, frescos y arañas de alabastro.

Questo hotel per così dire trasferisce l'Italia dal Mediterraneo all'Oceano Pacifico. Gli edifici sono stati eretti in stile toscano regalando all'ospite la sensazione di stare in mezzo ad una piazza italiana. Un campo da golf invita all'attività sportiva, mentre nell'area spa l'acqua gorgoglia lungo una parete alta tre piani, creando un dolce sottofondo acustico durante i massaggi e gli altri trattamenti di wellness. È particolarmente sontuosa la sala balli con il soffitto ornamentale, gli affreschi ed i lampadari d'alabastro.

Beige brown quarry stone, soft upholstery and a crackling fireplace create a cozy atmosphere.

Beigebrauner Naturstein, weiche Polstermöbel und knisterndes Kaminfeuer schaffen Gemütlichkeit.

Des pierres naturelles de couleur beige-marron, des meubles confortables et un feu de cheminée crépitant communiquent une atmosphère intime.

Piedra natural de tono marrón claro, mullidos muebles tapizados y fuego crujiente en la chimenea, garantizan la comodidad.

Pietre naturali di colore marrone chiaro, morbidi mobili imbottiti ed un fuoco scoppiettante nel camino creano l'ambiente confortevole.

Fountains and a pool radiate a nostalgic Mediterranean flair.

Springbrunnen und Pool verbreiten nostalgisches, mediterranes Flair.

Des jets d'eau et un parc répandent une ambiance méditerranéenne et nostalgique.

Las fuentes y la piscina transmiten un encanto mediterráneo, nostálgico.

Le fontane e la piscina diffondono un nostalgico fascino mediterraneo.

St. Regis Monarch Beach Resort & Spa *Dana Point, California* 27

Earthy and creamy hues ensure homeliness in the rooms.

Erdige und cremige Farbtöne sorgen für Behaglichkeit in den Zimmern.

Des tons crème et de terre communiquent une sensation de bien-être dans les chambres.

Tonalidades tierra y crema proporcionan comodidad y confort en las habitaciones.

Colori dai toni della terra e di crema creano l'atmosfera accogliente all'interno delle camere.

Mandarin Oriental Miami

Miami, Florida

All 327 rooms and 31 suites look over the Biscayne Bay, many also offer a view over the skyline of Miami. From the restaurant, the guest can watch the ships traveling through the bay. The suites let a hint of the Asian awareness of life arise: they have been designed in accordance with Feng-Shui criteria. Bamboo floors and rice-paper covered sliding walls are based on traditional Japanese architecture.

Alle 327 Zimmer und 31 Suiten schauen auf die Biscayne-Bucht, viele bieten dazu noch einen Blick auf die Skyline von Miami. Vom Restaurant aus kann der Gast die durch die Bucht fahrenden Schiffe beobachten. Die Suiten lassen einen Hauch von asiatischem Lebensgefühl aufkommen: Sie sind nach Feng-Shui-Kriterien gestaltet. Bambusboden und mit Reispapier bezogene Schiebewände basieren auf traditioneller japanischer Architektur.

Chacune des 327 chambres et des 31 suites donnent sur la baie de Biscayne, nombreuses sont celles qui permettent de jeter un regard sur les gratte-ciels de Miami. Du restaurant, l'hôte peut observer les bateaux circulant dans la baie. Les suites respirent l'art de vivre asiatique : Elles sont aménagées selon les critères du Feng-Shui. Les sols en bambous et les murs coulissants en papier de riz rappellent l'architecture japonaise traditionnelle.

Todas las 327 habitaciones y 31 suites tienen vista de la bahía Biscayne. Muchas ofrecen, además, vista del skyline de Miami. Desde el restaurante el huésped puede observar el movimiento de los barcos en la bahía. En las suites se respira un aire asiático: Están decoradas según los principios del Feng Shui. Los suelos de bambú y las paredes corredizas de papel de arroz se basan en la arquitectura tradicional japonesa.

Tutte le 327 camere e 31 suites guardano sulla baia di Biscayne, molte di esse offrono inoltre il panorama della skyline di Miami. Dal ristorante l'ospite può osservare le barche che attraversano la baia. Le suites regalano un pò della sensazione vita asiatica. Sono state create secondo i criteri di feng shui. I pavimenti di bambù e le pareti scorrevoli ricoperte di carta di riso sono basati sulla tradizionale architettura giapponese.

The Asian hotel group combines western and eastern elements both during the furnishing of the rooms and in the menu of the award-winning restaurant.

Sowohl bei der Einrichtung der Zimmer als auch bei der Speisekarte des preisgekrönten Restaurants kombiniert die asiatische Hotelgruppe westliche und fernöstliche Elemente.

La chaîne hôtelière asiatique combine des éléments occidentaux et orientaux et cela aussi bien au niveau de l'aménagement des chambres qu'au niveau des menus du restaurant plusieurs fois primé.

Tanto en la decoración de las habitaciones como en el menú del galardonado restaurante, el grupo hotelero asiático combina elementos del lejano Oriente con elementos occidentales.

Sia per quanto riguarda l'arredamento delle camere che anche il menu del ristorante premiato, il gruppo alberghiero asiatico combina elementi dell'Ovest e dell'Estremo Oriente.

Depending on the lighting conditions, the pool, bay, and sky merge into one optical unit.

Pool, Bucht und Himmel verschmelzen je nach Lichtstimmung zu einer optischen Einheit.

La piscine, la baie et le ciel se fondent selon la lumière dans la même unité optique.

La piscina, la bahia y el cielo se funden, según la luz del momento, en una unidad visual.

La piscina, la baia ed il cielo si confondono diventando un'unità ottica, secondo l'atmosfera della luce.

Extra-high ceilings, generous balconies, and Spanish marble in the bathrooms emphasize the luxurious furnishings of the suites.

Überhohe Decken, großzügige Balkone und spanischer Marmor in den Bädern unterstreichen die luxuriöse Ausstattung der Suiten.

Des plafonds particulièrement hauts, des balcons généreux et du marbre espagnol dans les sanitaires soulignent l'aménagement luxurieux des suites.

Techos muy altos, balcones amplios y mármol español en los baños, acentúan la lujosa decoración de las suites.

Soffitti altissimi, balconi spaziosi e marmo spagnolo nelle stanze da bagno sottolineano l'arredamento lussurioso delle suites.

The Ritz-Carlton, South Beach

Miami, Florida

Even though the estate lies in the midst of Miami's historical Art Deco district, it originates from the 50's of the past century; and the special flair of that era can still be felt today. The sweeping walls and stairs in the lobby and the pastel accents emanate a bright lightness, typical for the era when the building originated. The rooms of the hotel accommodate an extensive art collection, which includes works by Joan Miró.

Obwohl das Anwesen mitten in Miamis historischem Art déco-Bezirk liegt, stammt es aus den 50er Jahren des vergangenen Jahrhunderts; und das spezielle Flair dieser Zeit ist noch heute zu spüren. Geschwungene Wände und Treppen in der Lobby und pastellfarbene Akzente verbreiten eine heitere Leichtigkeit, wie sie zur Entstehungszeit des Baus typisch war. Die Räume des Hotels beherbergen eine umfangreiche Kunstsammlung, die auch Werke von Joan Miró einschließt.

Bien que la propriété soit située dans le quartier art déco du Miami historique, elle date des années 50 du siècle dernier ; et l'atmosphère particulière de cette époque est encore présente aujourd'hui. Des murs élancés et des escaliers dans les vestibules, ainsi que les teintes de couleur pastel répandent une joyeuse légèreté typique de l'époque du bâtiment. Les pièces de l'hôtel accueillent une collection d'art riche et variée possédant entre autre des œuvres de Joan Miró.

Aunque la mansión se encuentra en medio del distrito histórico Art Deco de Miami, su origen es de los años 50 del siglo pasado; y el encanto especial de aquella época se siente hoy todavía. Las paredes onduladas, las escaleras en el vestíbulo y los colores pasteles emanan una serena sutileza, típica de la época de su construcción. Los salones del hotel albergan una extensa colección de arte que, entre otras, incluye obras de Joan Miró.

Nonostante la tenuta si trovi in mezzo allo storico distretto art déco di Miami, l'hotel risale agli anni 50 del secolo scorso; ed il particolare fascino di quei tempi si sente ancora oggi. Pareti e scale dalle forme tondeggianti nella lobby e gli accenti dati dai colori pastelli diffondono una spensierata leggerezza tipica per il periodo in cui era stato costruito l'hotel. Nei vari locali dell'albergo si trova conservata una vasta collezione d'arte che comprende tra l'altro delle opere di Joan Miró.

Important parts of the furnishings have remained unchanged since the origin of the building.

Wichtige Teile der Ausstattung blieben seit der Entstehung des Baus unverändert.

Des parties importantes de l'aménagement sont restées inchangées depuis la construction du bâtiment.

Piezas importantes de la decoración han permanecido intactas desde la época de su construcción.

Importanti elementi dell'arredamento sono rimasti invariati dai tempi della costruzione dell'edificio.

For furnishing the 376 guestrooms and suites, only the very best materials were used: the furniture is made from genuine cherry wood.

Für die Ausstattung der 376 Gästezimmer und Suiten wurden nur allerfeinste Materialien verwendet: Die Möbel bestehen aus echtem Kirschholz.

Les matériaux les plus fins ont été utilisés pour aménager les 376 chambres d'hôte : les meubles sont fabriqués en bois de cerisier.

En la decoración de las 376 habitaciones y suites se emplearon exclusivamente los más finos materiales: Los muebles son de cerezo.

Per l'arredamento delle 376 camere e suites sono stati utilizzati esclusivamente materiali pregiatissimi. I mobili sono stati fatti di legno di ciliego autentico.

The Ritz-Carlton, South Beach *Miami, Florida* 39

The Breakers
Palm Beach, Florida

A house with tradition: The Breakers was already established in 1896; in its present shape it exists since 1926 at which time it was rebuilt after a fire. The architecture of the hotel is reminiscent of the Italian renaissance. 75 artists were brought from Italy to Palm Beach in order to paint the ceilings of the main lobby. Today the guests are looked after in 25 languages by a staff of 1800. Two golf courses, ten tennis places, 800 m private beach with view over the Atlantic invite to do sports.

Ein Haus mit Tradition: Bereits 1896 wurde das Breakers gegründet; in seiner heutigen Gestalt existiert es seit 1926, als es nach einem Brand wieder aufgebaut wurde. Die Architektur des Hotels erinnert an die italienische Renaissance. 75 Künstler wurden aus Italien nach Palm Beach geholt, um etwa die Decken in der Hauptlobby zu bemalen. Um die Gäste, die in über 25 Sprachen betreut werden, kümmern sich heute 1800 Angestellte. Zwei Golfplätze, zehn Tennisplätze und 800 m privater Strand mit Blick über den Atlantik laden zu sportlichen Aktivitäten ein.

Une maison à tradition : le Breakers fut fondé en 1896 ; dans l'état actuel, il existe depuis 1926, reconstruit après un incendie. L'architecture de l'hôtel rappelle la Renaissance italienne. 75 artistes originaires d'Italie furent invités à Palm Beach pour peindre les plafonds du salon principal. Aujourd'hui, 1800 employés s'occupent des clients de l'hôtel et cela en 25 langues étrangères différentes. Deux golfs, dix terrains de tennis et 800 m de plage privée avec vue sur l'Atlantique sont à disposition des clients pour les activités sportives.

Una casa con tradición: Ya en 1896 se fundó The Breakers; su apariencia actual la tiene desde 1926, después de haber sido reconstruido tras un incendio. La arquitectura del hotel evoca el renacimiento italiano. 75 artistas fueron traídos desde Italia para pintar los techos del vestíbulo principal. De los huéspedes, que son atendidos en más de 25 idiomas, se ocupan 1800 empleados. Dos campos de golf, diez canchas de tenis y 800 m de playa privada con vista al Atlántico, invitan a las actividades deportivas.

Una casa con tradizione: Già nel 1896 è stato fondato il Breakers; nella sua forma attuale esiste dal 1926 quando dopo un incendio è stato ricostruito. L'architettura dell'hotel ricorda il rinascimento italiano. 75 artisti sono stati portati dall'Italia a Palm Beach per decorare ad esempio i soffitti della lobby principale. Oggi 1800 dipendenti si occupano degli ospiti i quali sono seguiti in più di 25 lingue. Due campi da golf, dieci campi da tennis e 800 mt. di spiaggia privata con vista sull'Atlantico invitano a fare dello sport.

The architecture and the interior decoration were modelled on the *Villa Medici in Florence.*

Bei der Architektur und der Innenausstattung diente die *Villa Medici in Florenz* als Vorbild.

La Villa Médici de Florence a servie de modéle à l'architecture et l'aménagement intérieur.

Módelo para la arquitectura y la decoración interior fue la Villa Medici de Florencia.

La Villa Medici di Firenze serviva da modello per l'architettura e l'arredamento.

Palms and the architectural pomp in the style of the neo-renaissance ensure Mediterranean flair.

Palmen und bauliche Pracht im Stil der Neo-Renaissance sorgen für mediterranes Flair.

Les palmiers et la splendeur architecturale du bâtiment construit selon le style Néo-Renaissance donnent au lieu une touche méditerranéenne.

Las palmeras y el esplendor arquitectónico en estilo neo-renacentista proporcionan un encanto mediterráneo.

Palme e le costruzioni sfarzose nello stile del neo-rinascimento portano il fascino mediterraneo.

One&Only Ocean Club

Paradise Island, Bahamas

Several villas are spread across the hilly green spaces. Hibiscus and Bougainville shrubs line the path from the beach up to the terrace garden. It has been designed based on Versailles and decorated with European bronze and marble statues. At the highest point, the impressive arches from the 12th century Augustinian monastery arise. Mahogany beds, parquet floors and sisal mats provide the right mixture of elegance and casualness in the rooms and suites.

Mehrere Villen verteilen sich auf einer hügeligen Grünanlage. Hibiskus- und Bougainvilleasträucher säumen den Weg vom Strand hinauf zum Terrassengarten. Er ist nach dem Vorbild von Versailles angelegt und mit europäischen Bronze- und Marmorstatuen dekoriert. An der höchsten Stelle erheben sich die beeindruckenden Bögen der Ruine eines Augustinerklosters aus dem 12. Jahrhundert. In den Zimmern und Suiten sorgen Mahagonibetten, Parkettböden und Sisalteppiche für die richtige Mischung aus Eleganz und Lässigkeit.

Plusieurs villas sont dispersées sur une colline verdoyante. Des hibiscus et des buissons de bougainvilliers parsèment le chemin qui relie la plage aux jardins en terrasse. Celui-ci est dessiné sur le modèle de Versailles et est décoré de statues en bronze et en marbre. Sur le point culminant, s'élèvent les ruines d'un cloître augustin du 12ième siècle. Dans les chambres et les suites, l'assemblage élégant de lits en acajou, de parquets et de tapis en sisal assure un bon équilibre entre élégance et décontraction.

Varios chalés se distribuyen en el terreno con colinas. Hibiscos y buganvillas pueblan el camino que sube de la playa hacia el jardín de la terraza. Éste ha sido diseñado a semejanza de Versalles y decorado con estatuas europeas de bronce y de mármol. En la parte más alta se yerguen los impresionantes arcos de las ruinas de un claustro agustino del siglo XII. En las habitaciones y suites las camas de caoba, los suelos de parquet y las alfombras de sisal procuran la perfecta combinación de elegancia e informalidad.

Diverse ville si distribuiscono negli spazi verdi collinosi, cespugli d'ibisco e di bougainvillea contornano il sentiero dalla spiaggia fino ai giardini a terrazze. Sono stati creati sul modello di Versailles e decorati con sculture di bronzo e di marmo provenienti dall'Europa. Sul punto più alto s'innalzano le arcate dei resti di un monastero degli augustini del duecento. Nelle camere e suites i letti di mogano, il palquet ed i tappeti di sisal creano il giusto equilibrio tra eleganza e disinvoltura.

The rooms, suites, and public areas have been furnished and decorated with a love of detail.

Mit viel Liebe zum Detail sind die Zimmer, Suiten und öffentlichen Bereiche eingerichtet und dekoriert.

Les chambres, suites et espaces publics ont été décorés et aménagés dans l'amour du détail.

Las habitaciones, las suites y las áreas comunes están decoradas con mucho amor al detalle.

Le camere, le suites e le aree riservate al pubblico sono state create con molto amore per il dettaglio.

Eight villas in Balinese style and luxuriantly planted gardens in which the guests can let themselves be pampered under the sky belong to the spa.

Zum Spa gehören acht Villen im balinesischen Stil und üppig begrünte Gärten, in denen sich der Gast unter freiem Himmel verwöhnen lassen kann.

Huit villas dans le style balinéaire et dotées d'un vaste jardin font partie de l'espace spa, dans lequel l'hôte est invité à se laisser bichonner en plein air.

En el Spa se incluyen ocho chalés en estilo balinés y jardines exuberantes, en los cuales el huésped es mimado a cielo raso.

Fanno parte dell'area spa otto ville costruite nello stile balinese e giardini rigogliosamente verdi ove l'ospite si lascia viziare all'aperto.

Four Seasons Resort Great Exuma at Emerald Bay

Emerald Bay, Bahamas

The ocean is the main theme of this hotel. The guests have a private bathing inlet with a sandy white beach at their disposal, all 183 rooms have a view of Emerald Bay, and the house-own golf course leads along the coast over a dune landscape and mangrove protectorate up to a rocky peninsula. In the spa, one can enjoy massages under the sky, in which local natural salts along with indigenous herbs, blossoms, and oils are intended to relax the body.

Das Meer ist das zentrale Thema dieses Hotels. Den Gästen steht eine private Badebucht mit weißem Sandstrand zur Verfügung, alle 183 Zimmer bieten einen Blick auf die Emerald Bay, und der hauseigene Golfplatz führt entlang der Küste über Dünenlandschaften und Mangroven-Schutzgebiete bis zu einer felsigen Halbinsel. Im Spa kann man Massagen unter freiem Himmel genießen, bei der Natursalze aus örtlichen Vorkommen, heimische Kräuter, Blüten und Öle den Körper entspannen sollen.

La mer est le thème central de cet hôtel. Une baie de baignade privée au sable fin est mise à disposition des hôtes, toutes les 183 chambres ont vue sur l'Emerald Bay et le golf de la maison mène le long de la côte par un paysage de dunes et au travers de la zone de protection de mangroves à la presqu'île rocheuse. Dans l'espace spa, on peut apprécier les massages en plein air, où des sels naturels issus de gisements locaux, des herbes autochtones et des huiles permettent au corps de se détendre.

El mar es el motivo central de este hotel. Los huéspedes tienen a su disposición una bahía privada de arena blanca, todas las 183 habitaciones tienen vista de la Esmerald Bay, y el campo de golf proprio conduce a lo largo de la costa, pasando por paisajes de dunas y reservas naturales de manglares, a una península rocosa. En el Spa se puede disfrutar de masajes al aire libre, en los que se emplean sales naturales de yacimientos locales, hierbas de la región, flores y aceites, que ayudan a relajar el cuerpo.

Il mare costituisce il tema centrale di questo hotel. Una baia balneare privata con una spiaggia di sabbia bianca è a disposizione degli ospiti, tutte le 183 camere offrono la vista sull'Emerald Bay ed il campo da golf dell'albergo porta lungo la costa attraverso i paesaggi di dune e zone protette di mangrovi fino a una peninsula rocciosa. Nello spa si possono godere all'aperto i massaggi per i quali l'utilizzo di sali naturali, erbe, fiori ed olii di provenienza locale regala relax per il corpo.

The tasteful furnishings employ elements from colonial times.

Eine gediegene Einrichtung verwendet Elemente aus der Kolonialzeit.

Le robuste aménagement utilise des éléments originaires de l'époque coloniale.

Una decoración sutilmente elegante utiliza elementos de la época colonial.

Per l'arredamento accurato sono stati utilizzati elementi del periodo coloniale.

Sand, sun and saltwater—these "ingredients" are meant to ensure a restful vacation.

Sand, Sonne und Salzwasser – mit diesen drei „Zutaten" sollte ein erholsamer Urlaub sicher sein.

Du sable, du soleil et de l'eau salée – ces trois « ingrédients » assurent la réussite de vos vacances.

La arena, el sol y el agua de mar –con estos tres "ingredientes" las vacaciones deberían ser muy reconfortantes.

Sale, sole ed acque di mare – con questi tre "ingredienti" la vacanza rilassante dovrebbe essere assicurata.

Las Alamandas

Puerto Vallarta, Mexico

The actual luxury of this hotel is the complete silence and seclusion awaiting the guest. Only 14 suites are spread across grounds of over 1500 acres. A tropical park with lagoons and exotic birds tempt one to take long walks, a white beach to bathe in the pacific, and, whoever wants to travel with a private airplane will even find a hotel-own landing strip. The restaurant offers local specialties, whereby much of the fruit and vegetables are grown on the hotel premises.

Der eigentliche Luxus dieses Hotels ist die völlige Ruhe und Abgeschiedenheit, die den Gast erwartet. Nur 14 Suiten verteilen sich auf einem Gelände von über 600 Hektar. Eine tropische Parkanlage mit Lagunen und exotischen Vögeln lädt zu ausführlichen Spaziergängen ein, ein weißer Strand zum Baden im Pazifik, und wer mit dem Privatflugzeug anreisen möchte, findet sogar eine hoteleigene Landepiste vor. Das Restaurant bietet lokale Spezialitäten, wobei ein großer Teil des Obstes und Gemüses auf dem Hotelgelände angebaut wird.

Le vrai luxe de cet hôtel est la tranquillité et l'isolement total qui attendent l'hôte. 14 suites se partagent un terrain de plus de 600 hectares. Un parc tropical avec des lagunes et des oiseaux exotiques invitent à de longues promenades, une plage de sable fin à se baigner dans le Pacifique et celui qui veut arriver avec son avion privé, trouvera même une piste d'atterrissage propre à l'hôtel. Le restaurant propose des spécialités locales, la plupart des fruits et des légumes provenant du terrain de l'hôtel.

El verdadero lujo de este hotel son la total tranquilidad y aislamiento que esperan al huésped. Tan sólo 14 suites se encuentran repartidas en un área de más de 600 hectáreas. Un recinto tropical con lagunas y aves exóticas invita a hacer largos paseos; una playa blanca, a bañarse, y, el que quiere viajar con su avión particular, puede incluso aterrizar en la pista de aterrizaje del hotel. El restaurante ofrece especialidades de la región, entre las que se cuentan frutas y verduras que en gran parte se cultivan en el terreno del hotel.

Il vero lusso di questo hotel sta nell'assoluta tranquillità e solitudine che aspettano l'ospite. Solo 14 suites si distribuiscono su un terreno di 600 ettari. Il parco tropicale con lagune ed uccelli esotici invita a fare lunghe passeggiate, la spiaggia bianca invita a fare il bagno nel Pacifico e per chi volesse approdare con l'areo privato trova addirittura la pista di atterraggio privata dell'albergo. Il ristorante offre specialità locali per le quali una gran parte di frutta e verdura è coltivata nei campi propri dell'hotel.

*The **private beach** seems to be endless and offers a maximum of undisturbed recuperation.*

*Der **Privatstrand** scheint endlos zu sein und bietet ein Maximum an ungestörter Erholung.*

*La **plage privée** semble infinie et offre un maximum repos solitaire.*

*La **playa privada** parece infinita y proporciona el máximo descanso imaginable.*

*La **spiaggia privata** sembra non avere confini ed offre il massimo di un relax indisturbato.*

*The **powerful** fresh colors are a hallmark of the hotel.*
*Die **kräftigen** frischen Farben sind ein Markenzeichen des Hotels.*
*Les **couleurs** franches et fraîches sont la marque de fabrique de l'hôtel.*
*Los **colores** fuertes y vivaces son una característica del hotel.*
*I **colori** forti e freschi rappresentano la caratteristica dell'hotel.*

Four Seasons Resort Punta Mita

Punta Mita, Mexico

The visitor can purvey an unobstructed view of the white sand beach of which a long section is reserved for the hotel guests from each of the 140 guestrooms. The golf course also grants a view of the ocean. In the spa the guest can let himself be pampered with a special massage in which not only local sage oil but also tequila is used. The hotel offers a special entertainment program for children of five to twelve.

Von allen 140 Gästezimmern aus kann der Besucher den Blick ungehindert über den weißen Sandstrand schweifen lassen, von dem ein langer Abschnitt ausschließlich den Hotelgästen zur Verfügung steht. Auch der Golfplatz gewährt eine Aussicht aufs Meer. Im Spa kann sich der Gast mit einer speziellen Massage verwöhnen lassen, bei der nicht nur einheimisches Salbeiöl, sondern auch Tequila zum Einsatz kommt. Für Kinder von fünf bis zwölf Jahren bietet das Hotel ein besonderes Unterhaltungsprogramm.

De toutes les 140 chambres d'hôte, le visiteur peut laisser errer son regard sur la plage de sable blanc, dont une grande partie est réservée exclusivement aux clients de l'hôtel. Le golf a aussi vue sur la mer. Dans le secteur spa, l'hôte peut goûter les bienfaits d'un massage spécial, au cours duquel non seulement de l'huile de sauge locale mais aussi de la Tequila sont utilisés. L'hôtel offre aux enfants âgés entre cinq et douze ans un programme spécial de divertissement.

Desde todas las 140 habitaciones los huéspedes pueden disfrutar de la vista de la playa de arena blanca, de la cual una gran parte es de uso exclusivo para los huéspedes del hotel. También desde el campo de golf se tiene vista al mar. En el Spa el huésped es exquisitamente tratado con un masaje especial, en el que no sólo se utilizan aceites de salvia de la región, sino también tequila. Para niños entre los cinco y los doce años el hotel ofrece un programa especial de recreación.

Da tutte le 140 camere, gli ospiti possono lasciar scorrere l'occhio liberamente sulla spiaggia di sabbia bianca della quale un lungo pezzo è riservato esclusivamente agli ospiti dell'albergo. Pure il campo da golf concede la vista sul mare. Nello spa l'ospite può gradire un massaggio speciale per il quale non si utilizza soltanto l'olio di salvia locale, ma anche la tequila. L'hotel offre un programma di divertimento speciale per i bambini dai cinque ai dodici anni.

The sea is present everywhere. The nearby coral reefs provide the beach with white sand.

Das Meer ist überall präsent. Nahe gelegene Korallenriffe sorgen für weißen Sand am Strand.

La mer est partout présente. Les récifs de corail voisins assure la blancheur du sable des plages.

El mar es omnipresente. Gracias a los cercanos arrecifes coralinos la arena de la playa es blanca.

Il mare è presente ovunque. Le barriere coralline presenti in vicinanza fanno diventare bianca la sabbia della spiaggia.

The epitome of luxury is not pomposity here, but the unique view.

Inbegriff für Luxus ist hier nicht Prunk, sondern die einmalige Aussicht.

Le luxe ici n'est pas ostentatoire ; ce qui est luxueux ici, c'est la vue imprenable.

Aquí la quintaesencia del lujo no es la suntuosidad sino la excepcional vista.

Qui la quintessenza del lusso non è soltanto lo sfarzo, ma anche l'eccezionale panorama.

El Tamarindo

Costalegre, Mexico

29 beach, park, and forest villas are spread across a terrain of over 2000 acres. The individual buildings are openly designed; only the bedrooms were put under the roof as a room within a room. Each villa has its own small pool. A world-class golf course belongs to the hotel, distinguished by its scenic variety. From the dense forest, over the hilly park and up to the steep cliffs and private sand beaches, everything can be found here.

29 Strand-, Park- und Waldvillen verteilen sich über ein Gelände von über 800 Hektar. Die einzelnen Gebäude sind offen gestaltet, nur der Schlafraum wurde als Raum im Raum unter das große Dach gestellt. Jede Villa hat einen eigenen kleinen Pool. Zum Hotel gehört ein Weltklasse-Golfplatz, der sich besonders durch landschaftliche Vielfältigkeit auszeichnet. Vom dichten Wald, über hügelige Parkanlagen bis hin zu steilen Klippen und privaten Sandstränden ist hier alles zu finden.

29 villas au bord de la plage, du parc ou de la forêt se partagent un terrain de plus de 800 hectares. Chaque bâtiment est construit de façon ouverte, seule la chambre à coucher est située sous le toit, comme espace dans l'espace. Chaque villa a sa petite piscine privée. L'hôtel possède un golf de première qualité, connu par la diversité de ses paysages. On y trouve de tout, de la forêt profonde aux collines vertes, en passant par des falaises à pic et des plages privées.

29 chalés en la playa, en los jardines y en el bosque, se encuentran en un terreno de más de 800 hectáreas. La arquitectura de cada construcción es abierta, solamente el dormitorio se encuentra como un espacio dentro del espacio bajo el gran techo. Cada chalé tiene su propia piscina pequeña. El hotel cuenta con un campo de golf de primera que se caracteriza por la variedad de sus paisajes. Desde bosques espesos, pasando por jardines ondulados, hasta escarpados peñascos y playas privadas, nada falta.

29 ville sulla spiaggia, nel parco e nel bosco si distribuiscono su un terreno di 800 ettari. I singoli edifici sono stati creati in modo aperto, solo la stanza da letto è stata inserita sotto il grande tetto, come stanza nella stanza. Ogni villa ha la sua piscina. Fa parte dell'hotel un campo da golf di rango mondiale e che è caratterizzato in particolare dalla sua varietà paesistica. Dal fitto bosco, attraverso i parchi collinosi fino ai ripidi scogli e le spiagge private – qui si trova di tutto.

The guests are accommodated in individual houses, partially in tropical woodlands, partially near the beach.

Die Gäste sind in einzelnen Häusern untergebracht, die teils in einer tropischen Waldlandschaft, teils nahe am Strand liegen.

Les clients sont logés dans les différentes maisons situées soit dans un paysage de forêt tropicale et soit à proximité de la plage.

Los huéspedes se alojan en casas individuales, que en parte están situadas en el bosque tropical, en parte cerca de la playa.

Gli ospiti sono alloggiati in singole case che si trovano in parte nel paesaggio di un bosco tropicale ed in parte vicino alla spiaggia.

Much wood and the palm-frond covered roofs contribute to the nature-like atmosphere.

Viel Holz und palmwedelgedeckte Dächer tragen zur naturnahen Atmosphäre bei.

Beaucoup de bois et les toits recouverts de palmes participent à créer une atmosphère naturelle.

Mucha madera y tejados cubiertos de hojas de palmera contribuyen a un ambiente natural.

L'utilizzo di molto legno ed i tetti ricoperti di rami di palme contribuiscono all'atmosfera naturale.

Ikal del Mar

Riviera Maya, Mexico

"Respect nature" is the motto of this boutique resort north of Playa del Carmen. Its 29 villas are intended to visually melt into the surrounding jungle; the paths were laid out so that no older tree had to give way. It winds in a meandering form through the estate. At night, the outdoor facilities are not illuminated with artificial light that could disturb the view of the starry sky, but with torches. All the villas were erected with wood and stone from the region.

Respekt vor der Natur ist das Motto dieses Boutique-Resorts nördlich von Playa del Carmen. Seine 29 Villen sollen optisch mit dem umgebenden Dschungel verschmelzen; die Wege wurden so angelegt, dass kein alter Baum weichen musste. Sie winden sich mäanderförmig durch das Anwesen. Bei Nacht werden die Außenanlagen nicht mit Kunstlicht beleuchtet, das den Blick auf den Sternenhimmel stören könnte, sondern mit Fackeln. Alle Villen wurden mit Holz und Stein aus der Region errichtet.

Le respect de la nature est le thème de ce domaine-boutique, au Nord de Playa del Carmen. Ses 29 villas doivent se noyer optiquement dans la jungle environnante ; Les chemins ont été tracés de façon à préserver les vieux arbres. Ils dessinent un méandre au travers de la propriété. Le soir, les espaces extérieurs ne sont pas éclairés artificiellement mais par des flambeaux afin de ne pas gêner l'œil perdu dans la contemplation des étoiles. Toutes les villas ont été construites à partir du bois et des pierres de la région.

El lema de este resort tipo boutique al norte de Playa del Carmen es el respeto por la naturaleza. Sus 29 chalés se funden visualmente con la selva que los rodea. Los senderos que serpentean a través del recinto, están diseñados de tal manera que no hubo necesidad de remover ningún árbol antiguo. Por la noche las zonas exteriores se iluminan con antorchas y no con luz artificial, ya que ésta podría perturbar la vista del cielo lleno de estrellas. Todos los chalés han sido construidos en madera y piedra de la región.

Il rispetto per la natura costituisce il motto di questo boutique-resort a Nord della Playa del Carmen. Le sue 29 ville vogliono confondersi otticamente con la giungla circostante; i sentieri sono stati tracciati in modo che nessun albero vecchio dovesse essere tolto. S'intrecciano a meandri attraverso la tenuta. Di notte gli impianti esterni non sono illuminati con la luce artificiale che potrebbe disturbare lo sguardo nel cielo stellato, ma con le fiaccole. Tutte le ville sono state fatte di legno e pietra locali.

In complete seclusion in the middle of nature, such elementary things as sun, wind, and shade can be consciously experienced.

In völliger Zurückgezogenheit, mitten in der Natur, lassen sich so elementare Dinge wie Sonne, Wind und Schatten bewusst erleben.

Dans un isolement total, au milieu de la nature, des choses aussi élémentaires telles que le soleil, le vent et l'ombre deviennent perceptibles.

En el total aislamiento en medio de la naturaleza se viven a conciencia las cosas más elementales: El sol, el viento y la sombra.

In assoluta solitudine, in mezzo alla natura, le cose elementarie come il sole, il vento e l'ombra si possono sperimentare con tutti i sensi.

Pure relaxation, *regardless of whether in bed in the romantic mosquito net, in the hammock, or at the refreshing pool in front of the private veranda.*

Entspannung pur, *egal ob im Bett mit romantischem Moskitonetz, in der Hängematte oder am Erfrischungspool vor der privaten Veranda.*

La détente pure, *que vous soyez dans un lit protégé par une moustiquaire romantique, dans un hamac ou la piscine fraîche située devant votre véranda privée.*

Relajamiento puro: *En la cama con romántico mosquitero, en la hamaca, o en la piscina frente al propio porche.*

Relax puro, *sia al letto provvisto di una romantica zanzariera, sia nell'amaca oppure lungo la piscina di fronte alla veranda privata.*

"Ikal del Mar" *translated means "Poetry of the Sea." Each luxurious hut is dedicated to a different poet.*

„Ikal del Mar" *bedeutet übersetzt „Poesie des Meeres". Jede Luxushütte des Resorts ist einem anderen Dichter gewidmet.*

« Ikal del Mar » *signifie « poésie de la mer ». Chaque cabane de luxe du domaine est dédiée à un poète.*

"Ikal del Mar" *significa "poesía del mar". Todas las cabañas de lujo del resort están dedicadas a un poeta diferente.*

"Ikal del Mar" *significa tradotto "poesie del mare". Ogni capanna di lusso del resort è dedicata ad un altro poeta.*

One&Only Palmilla

Los Cabos, Mexico

Desert and ocean meet at the southern tip of Baja California. Including restaurants, lounge, and pool, the 173 lodgings in the luxury resort lie completely secluded between the hills of a peninsula. Their whitewashed walls and red tiled roofs are modeled after the village building tradition. It wants for nothing, there is even an own chapel. Great credit is due the peacefulness and view of the especially beautiful sea. Also, grey whales can be seen offshore in winter.

An der Südspitze von Baja California treffen Wüste und Meer aufeinander. Völlig abgeschieden liegen die 173 Unterkünfte des Luxusresorts zusammen mit Restaurants, Lounge und Pool zwischen den Hügeln einer Halbinsel. Ihre weiß gekalkten Wände und die roten Ziegeldächer sind der lokalen dörflichen Bautradition nachempfunden. Es mangelt an nichts, es gibt sogar eine eigene Kapelle. Größte Pluspunkte sind die Ruhe und der Blick aufs Meer, das hier besonders schön ist. Im Winter sind zudem Grauwale vor der Küste zu sehen.

A la pointe Sud de Baja California, la mer et le désert se rencontrent. Les 173 logements de ce domaine de luxe ainsi que les restaurants, salons et piscines sont complètement isolés entre les collines de la presqu'île. Les murs blanchis à la chaux et leurs toits de tuiles rouges rappellent l'architecture locale traditionnelle. Il ne lui manque rien puisqu'il a même une chapelle. Ce qui fait vraiment la différence ce sont la tranquillité et la vue sur la mer, particulièrement belle ici. En hiver, des baleines grises sont visibles depuis la côte.

En la punta sur de Baja California se encuentran el mar y el desierto. Entre las colinas de una península se encuentran, en total aislamiento, las 173 habitaciones de este resort de lujo, junto con restaurantes, lounge y piscina. Las paredes encaladas y los tejados de tejas rojas siguen la tradición local de construcción. No falta nada, incluso hay una capilla propia. Las grandes ventajas son la paz y la vista del mar, que aquí es especialmente hermoso. En invierno, además, se pueden observar las ballenas grises.

Sulla punta meridionale della Baja California s'incontrano deserto e mare. I 173 alloggi del resort di lusso insieme a ristoranti, lounge e piscina si trovano in assoluta solitudine in mezzo alle colline di una peninsula. I muri intonacati di bianco ed i tetti ricoperti di tegole rosse hanno preso spunto dalla tradizione costruttiva locale. Non manca niente, è presente addirittura una capella privata. I punti di maggiore vantaggio sono la tranquillità ed il panorama sul mare che qui è particolarmente bello. Durante l'inverno si possono inoltre osservare delle balenottere grigie in vicinanza alla costa.

Desert and coast: One cannot always swim here, as the surf is often too strong.

Wüste und Küste: Nicht immer kann man hier baden, da die Brandung oft sehr stark ist.

Le désert et la côte : il n'est pas toujours possible de prendre un bain, le ressac étant souvent trop fort.

Desierto y costa: No siempre puede uno bañarse aquí ya que el oleaje es a menudo muy fuerte.

Deserto e costa: Non sempre qui si può fare il bagno, essendo spesso presente una risacca molto forte.

In the blue hour, *when the sun descends, the lighting scenery of the contemporarily designed restaurant stands out.*

In der blauen Stunde, *wenn die Sonne untergeht, kommt die Lichtinszenierung des zeitgenössisch gestalteten Restaurants zur Geltung.*

A l'heure bleue, *au moment du crépuscule, la mise en scène lumineuse du restaurant à l'architecture contemporaine montre tout son faste.*

A la hora *de la puesta del sol resalta especialmente la iluminación del restaurante diseñado en un estilo contemporáneo.*

Durante l'ora blu, *al tramonto del sole, la messa in scena dell'illuminazione del ristorante disegnato in modo contemporaneo trova la sua valorizzazione.*

The accommodations *are located in one- to three-floor buildings, surrounded by palm trees and tropical blossoms.*

In ein- bis dreigeschossigen *Gebäuden liegen die Unterkünfte, die von Palmen und tropischen Blüten umgeben sind.*

Les logements *sont situés dans des bâtiments de un à trois étages entourés de palmes et de fleurs tropicales.*

En construcciones *de uno hasta tres pisos se ubican las habitaciones, rodeadas de palmeras y flores tropicales.*

Gli alloggi *si trovano in edifici da uno a tre piani, contornati da palme e fiori esotici.*

Las Ventanas al Paraiso
Los Cabos, Mexico

Whoever enters this hotel is tempted never to leave it during the entire stay. Besides a rimless pool, a sand beach, tennis, golf, snorkeling and fishing, it also offers individual yoga courses and aroma massages under the sky. Open fire, marble showers and whirlpools create a relaxed atmosphere in the 61 suites. Patios that cannot be seen into in the beach suites invite to cooling in a private whirlpool daytime, while nights the starry sky can be watched with a telescope.

Wer dieses Hotel betritt, ist versucht, es während des ganzen Aufenthalts nicht mehr zu verlassen. Es bietet nicht nur einen randlosen Pool, Zugang zum Sandstrand, Tennis-, Golf-, Schnorchel- und Angelmöglichkeiten, sondern auch Yogakurse und Aromamassagen unter freiem Himmel. In den 61 Suiten schaffen Kaminfeuer, Marmorduschen und Whirlpool eine entspannte Atmosphäre. Nicht einsehbare Terrassen in den Strand-Suiten laden tagsüber zu einer Abkühlung im privaten Whirlpool ein, während sich nachts mit einem Teleskop der Sternenhimmel beobachten lässt.

Celui qui rentrera dans cet hôtel, ne pourra plus le quitter de tout le séjour. Il offre non seulement une piscine sans bord mais aussi un accès à une plage de sable et à de nombreux sports comme de tennis, de golf, d'apnée et de pêche à la ligne, ainsi que des cours de yoga et des massages aromatiques en plein air. Dans les 61 suites, le feux de bois, la douche en marbre et le jacuzzi créent une ambiance de détente. Dans les suites, côté plage, des terrasses invisibles permettent de se rafraîchir, dans la journée, dans la piscine privée et, la nuit venue, d'observer au télescope le ciel étoilé.

Quien pone el pie en este hotel, tratará de no dejarlo mientras dure su estadía. No sólo ofrece una piscina sin bordes, acceso a la playa, tenis, golf, buceo con snórkel y pesca, sino también cursos individuales de yoga y masajes aromáticos al aire libre. El fuego de la chimenea, las duchas de mármol y el jacuzzi proporcionan en las 61 suites un relajado ambiente de descanso. Terrazas ocultas en las suites de la playa invitan de día a refrescarse en el jacuzzi, mientras que por la noche se puede observar el firmamento con un telescopio.

Chiunque entri in questo hotel, cercerà di non uscirne più durante tutto il soggiorno. Non solo l'hotel offre una piscina senza bordi, l'accesso alla spiaggia di sabbia, campi da tennis e da golf, la possibilità di fare l'immersione con lo snorkel e di andare a pesca, ma anche corsi individuali di yoga e massaggi aromatici all'aperto. Nelle 61 suites, il fuoco del camino, docce fatte in marmo e la vasca ad idromassaggio creano un'atmosfera rilassante. Terrazze riparate dallo sguardo nelle suites sulla spiaggia invitano a rinfrescarsi durante il giorno nella vasca ad idromassaggio privata, mentre di notte si può osservare il cielo stellato con un telescopio.

Like a small village with narrow lanes, stairs, and squares, the hotel facility offers great variety.

Wie ein kleines Dorf mit Gassen, Treppen und Plätzen angelegt, bietet die Hotelanlage viel Abwechslung.

Le domaine de l'hôtel est construit comme un petit village avec ses ruelles, ses escaliers et ses places et offre une diversité d'activités.

Las instalaciones del hotel ofrecen la variedad de una pequeña aldea, con sus callejuelas, escaleras y plazas.

Come un piccolo paese con vicoli, scale e piazze, l'impianto dell'hotel offre molta varietà.

The interior in Spanish-Mexican style lives from the natural materials.

Das Interieur im spanisch-mexikanischen Stil lebt von natürlichen Materialien.

L'intérieur, aménagé dans le style mexico-ibérique, vit des matériaux naturels qui le constituent.

El interior en un estilo español-mejicano, vive de los materiales naturales.

Gli arredamenti interni nello stile spagnolo-messicano vivono dall'utilizzo di materiali naturali.

The facility architecture combines simple white cubes with sun shielding verandas made of wood and straw.

Die Architektur der Anlage kombiniert schlichte weiße Kuben mit Sonnenschutzveranden aus Holz und Stroh.

L'architecture du domaine combine des cubes blancs et lisses avec des vérandas en bois et en paille protégées du soleil.

La arquitectura del conjunto combina sencillos cubos blancos con porches cubiertos de madera y paja.

L'architettura dell'impianto combina semplici cubi bianchi con verande parasole fatte di legno e paglia.

Grand Hôtel du Cap-Ferrat

Cap Ferrat, France

Not every hotel can boast of a royal past. The Grand Hotel du Cap Ferrat, however, lies on an estate that belonged to the Belgian Prince Leopold II in the 19th century. Even today, the premises spaciousness is impressive. The swimming pool awaits one with its special extra: it does not only have the size of an Olympic swimming pool and offers a view of the sea, but is filled with saltwater that is warmed up to a pleasant temperature.

Nicht jedes Hotel kann sich einer königlichen Vergangenheit rühmen. Das Grand Hotel du Cap Ferrat jedoch liegt auf einem Anwesen, das im 19. Jahrhundert dem belgischen Prinzen Leopold II. gehörte. Noch heute beeindruckt das Gelände durch seine Weitläufigkeit. Der Swimmingpool wartet mit einem speziellen Extra auf: Er besitzt nicht nur die Größe der olympischen Schwimmbecken und bietet einen Blick über das Meer, sondern ist mit Salzwasser gefüllt, das auf angenehme Temperaturen erwärmt wird.

Rares sont les hôtels qui possèdent un passé royal. Le Grand Hôtel du Cap Ferrat est situé sur le domaine qui appartenait au 19ième siècle au prince belge Léopold II. Le bâtiment impressionne aujourd'hui encore par son étendue. La piscine vous réserve bien des surprises : Non seulement elle a la taille d'un bassin olympique mais elle offre aussi une belle vue sur la mer et est remplie par de l'eau de mer chauffée à une température agréable.

No cualquier hotel puede vanagloriarse de tener un pasado real. Pero el Grand Hotel du Cap Ferrat sí puede, ya que se encuentra en una mansión que perteneció al príncipe belga Leopoldo II en el siglo XIX. Aun hoy impresiona el recinto por su amplitud. La piscina ofrece una atracción extra: No sólo tiene el tamaño de una piscina olímpica y ofrece vista al mar, sino que además es de agua de mar agradablemente climatizada.

Non tutti gli hotel si possono vantare di un passato reale. Il Grand Hotel du Cap Ferrat invece si trova su una tenuta che nel dicianovesimo secolo apparteneva al principe belga Leopoldo II. Ancora oggi la tenuta è impressionante per la sua vasta dimensione. La piscina offre una particolarità: Non solo ha dimensioni di una vasca olimpionica ed offre il panorama sul mare, ma è riempito d'acqua di mare che viene riscaldata per raggiungere temperature gradevoli.

The rooms exude tasteful leisureliness, the hotel foyer a Mediterranean flair.

Die Zimmer verbreiten gediegene Gemütlichkeit, die Hotelhalle mediterranes Flair.

Les chambres respirent un noble confort, le hall de l'hôtel une atmosphère méditerranéenne.

Las habitaciones irradian una elegante comodidad, el vestibulo el encanto mediterráneo.

Le camere diffondono un'atmosfera d'accurata accoglienza, la lobby invece il fascino mediterraneo.

84 Grand Hôtel du Cap-Ferrat *Cap Ferrat, France*

From the swimming pool, the guest can peruse the Mediterranean.

Vom Swimmingpool aus kann der Gast den Blick über das Mittelmeer schweifen lassen.

Depuis la piscine, l'hôte peut laisser errer son regard sur la mer Méditerranée.

Desde la piscina el huésped puede descansar la vista sobre el Mediterráneo.

Dalla piscina l'ospite può lasciar scorrere l'occhio sul Mare Mediterraneo.

Danai Beach Resort
Chalkidiki, Greece

The hotel facility snuggles the steep cliffs of the Aegean coast, named after beautiful Danai, a lover of Zeus, the father of the gods in Greek mythology. The individual villas are surrounded by pine groves, offering a number of pleasantly shaded spots. The buildings accommodate 55 rooms and six suites. Marble bathrooms and floors are standard, in some suites there are still even marble fireplaces, letting the guest have the day come to an end in front of a crackling fire.

An die steilen Klippen der ägäischen Küste schmiegt sich die Hotelanlage, die nach der schönen Danai benannt ist, in der griechischen Mythologie eine Geliebte des Göttervaters Zeus. Die einzelnen Villen sind von einem Pinienhain umgeben, der eine Reihe angenehm schattiger Plätze bietet. Die Gebäude beherbergen 55 Zimmer und sechs Suiten. Marmorbad und -böden gehören zum Standard, in einigen Suiten gibt es sogar noch einen Marmorkamin, vor dem der Gast den Tag bei einem prasselnden Feuer ausklingen lassen kann.

Le domaine de l'hôtel est accroché aux rochers escarpés du littoral de la mer Egée. Celui-ci porte le nom de la belle Danaé, une des maîtresses du roi des dieux, Zeus, dans la mythologie grecque. Les différentes villas sont entourées d'un bosquet de pins parasol qui offre une série de clairières ombragées bien agréables. Les bâtiments contiennent 55 chambres et six suites. Les salles de bains et les sols en marbre font partie de l'installation standard ; certaines suites ont même une cheminée en marbre qui permet à l'hôte de commencer la journée devant un feu crépitant.

Sobre los escarpados acantilados de la costa egea se recuesta el hotel, que lleva el nombre de la bella Danai, una amante de Zeus, padre de los dioses, según la mitología griega. Los chalés individuales están rodeados de un bosque de pinos que procuran lugares agradables de sombra. El complejo alberga 55 habitaciones y seis suites. Baños y suelos de mármol son estándar, en algunas suites incluso hay una chimenea de mármol, ante la cual, con fuego crepitante, el huésped puede terminar el día.

L'impianto dell'hotel che è denominato secondo la bella Danai – nella mitologia greca un'amante del dio padre Zeus – si stringono ai ripidi scogli della costa egea. Le singole ville sono contornate di un bosco di pini marittimi che offre una serie di posti gradevolmente ombreggiati. Gli edifici alloggiano 55 camere e sei suites. Il bagno ed il suo pavimento fatti di marmo fanno parte dello standard, alcune suites dispongono addirittura di un camino di marmo davanti al quale l'ospite può concludere la giornata con un fuoco scoppiettante.

The elevated facility offers a panoramic view of the Mediterranean.

Die erhöht gelegene Anlage bietet einen Panoramablick über das Mittelmeer.

Le domaine situé en hauteur offre une vue panoramique sur la mer Méditerranée.

La ubicación del hotel en lo alto permite una vista panorámica del mar Mediterráneo.

L'impianto che si trova in posizione rialzata offre il panorama sul Mare Mediterraneo.

The opulent room furnishings will leave no wish unfulfilled.

Die opulente Ausstattung der Räume dürfte keinen Wunsch offen lassen.

L'opulence de l'aménagement des espaces ne devrait pas laisser de désir non exaucé.

La opulenta decoración de las habitaciones satisface todos los deseos.

Gli arredi sontuosi delle camere non dovrebbero lasciare niente da desiderare.

Blue Palace Resort & Spa

Crete, Greece

On the northern coast of Crete, three kilometers from the next town, one can find peace and seclusion in the Blue Palace. Its 204 rooms and suites are spread across several individual bungalows embedded in the cliffs so the guest can enjoy the view of the Mediterranean from above. Treatments are offered in the spa using pure seawater. Those who have then worked up an appetite for swimming can drive down to the hotel's own 200-meter beach in a panorama elevator.

An der Nordostküste von Kreta, drei Kilometer vom nächsten Ort entfernt, lassen sich im Blue Palace Ruhe und Abgeschiedenheit finden. Seine 204 Zimmer und Suiten sind auf mehrere, in die Klippen eingebettete Einzelbungalows verteilt, sodass der Gast von oben die Aussicht über das Mittelmeer genießen kann. Im Spa werden Behandlungen mit reinem Meerwasser angeboten. Wer dadurch Lust zum Baden bekommen hat, kann mit einem Panoramaaufzug hinunter zum 200 Meter langen hoteleigenen Strand fahren.

Sur le côte nord-est de la Crète, à trois kilomètres du prochain village, vous trouverez le calme et l'isolement au Blue Palace. Ses 204 chambres et suites sont situées dans plusieurs bungalows individuels accrochés à la falaise, à partir de laquelle l'hôte peut apprécier la vue sur la mer Méditerranée. Dans le service spa, des traitements à l'eau de mer pure sont proposés. Celui qui éprouve le désir d'aller se baigner après peut accéder par un ascenseur panoramique à la plage privée de l'hôtel longue de 200 mètres.

En la costa noreste de Creta, a tres kilómetros de distancia del lugar más próximo, se encuentran la paz y el aislamiento en el Blue Palace. Sus 204 habitaciones y suites se encuentran repartidas en los bungalows independientes, incrustados en los peñascos, de tal forma que el huésped puede disfrutar desde lo alto de la vista sobre el Mediterráneo. En el Spa se ofrecen tratamientos con agua de mar. Y a quien se sienta animado a nadar, puede bajar en ascensor con vista panorámica a la playa privada del hotel, de 200 metros de largo.

Sulla costa a nord-est di Creta, distante tre chilometri dal prossimo paese, nel Blue Palace si trova tranquillità e solitudine. Le sue 204 camere e suites sono distribuite su diverse villette singole che si stringono agli scogli in modo che l'ospite possa godersi il panorama dall'alto sul Mare Mediterraneo. Nello spa sono offerti trattamenti con acqua di mare pura. A chi ora è venuta la voglia di fare un bagno, può scendere al mare con un ascensore panoramico, fino alla spiaggia privata dell'hotel lunga 200 mt.

Whether in the roofed-over swimming pool, in the open-air pool, or directly in the sea: the guests can swim in any kind of weather.

Ob im überdachten Schwimmbecken, im Open-Air-Pool oder direkt im Meer: Die Gäste können bei jedem Wetter baden.

Que ce soit dans le bassin couvert, dans le bassin en plein air ou directement dans la mer : les hôtes peuvent se baigner quelque soit le temps.

Sea en la piscina cubierta, en la piscina abierta o directamente en el mar: Los huéspedes pueden bañarse, no importa el tiempo que haga.

Sia nella piscina coperta, sia nella piscina all'aria aperta o direttamente in mare: gli ospiti possono fare il bagno con qualsiasi tempo.

One seldom finds such relatively modern architecture and furnishings as in the Blue Palace on Crete.

Eine relativ moderne Architektur und Ausstattung wie die des Blue Palace findet man selten auf Kreta.

Il est rare de trouver sur Crète une architecture et un aménagement aussi moderne qu'au Blue Palace.

Una arquitectura y una decoración relativamente modernas, como en el Blue Palace, son poco comunes en Creta.

L'architettura e l'arredamento relativamente moderni del Blue Palace si trovano solo raramente sull'isola di Creta.

Park Hyatt Goa Resort & Spa

Goa, India

The Indo-Portuguese bungalows are grouped village-like around the waterways and sparkling lagoons in south Goa—but are so ably arranged that no house blocks the view of another. In front of the door, the Arrossim Beach spreads out like a large white towel. Antiques, colonial artifacts, and noble materials reflect Goa's rich cultural heritage. Outdoor showers are hidden between palm trees and ferns. And in the beauty pavilions, Ayurveda massages let all hectic be forgotten.

Wie ein Dorf gruppieren sich die indo-portugiesischen Bungalows um Wasserstraßen und glitzernde Lagunen im Süden Goas – und sind dabei so geschickt verteilt, dass kein Haus dem anderen die Sicht verstellt. Vor der Tür breitet sich der Arrossim Beach wie ein großes, weißes Handtuch aus. Antiquitäten, koloniale Artefakte und edle Materialien reflektieren Goas reiches kulturelles Erbe. Outdoor-Duschen verstecken sich zwischen Palmen und Farnen. Und in den Beauty-Pavillons lassen Ayurveda-Massagen alle Hektik vergessen.

Les bungalows indo-portugais sont regroupés comme dans un village autour des voies navigables et des lagunes scintillantes au Sud de Goa – et sont cependant disposées de telle manière à ce que chacune est une vue dégagée. Devant la porte, s'étend la Arrossim Beach comme une grosse serviette blanche. Les antiquités, les artéfacts de l'époque coloniale et les matériaux précieux renvoient au riche héritage culturel de Goa. Les douches en plein air se cachent entre les palmiers et les fougères. Dans les pavillons-Beauty, les massages ayurvédiques viennent à bout de tous les stress.

Como en una aldea los bungalows indo-portugueses se agrupan en torno a los canales y las lagunas centelleantes en el sur de Goa, estando distribuidas de manera tan hábil que ninguna edificación le estropea la vista a otra. Ante la puerta se extiende la playa de Arrossim como una gran sábana blanca. Las antigüedades, los artefactos coloniales y los materiales nobles reflejan la rica herencia cultural de Goa. Las duchas al aire libre se esconden entre palmeras y helechos. Y en los salones de belleza los masajes de Ayurveda ayudan a olvidar las prisas.

Come in un paese, le villette nello stile indo-portughese si raggruppano attorno a vie d'acqua e scintillanti lagune nel Sud di Goa – e sono state disposte in modo così abile che nessuna casa disturba la vista dell'altra. Davanti alla porta l'Arrossim Beach si estende come un grande telo bianco. Antichità, artefatti coloniali e materiali pregiati rispecchiano la ricca eredità di Goa. Docce all'esterno si nascondono tra palme e felci. Nei beauty-pavillons i massaggi ayurveda fanno dimenticare tutto lo stress.

Exotic beauties in a marble bath, swimming candles, and architectural effects testify to the attention paid to detail.

Exotische Schönheiten im Marmor-Bad, Schwimmkerzen und architektonische Effekte beweisen die Liebe zum Detail.

Les beautés exotiques dans les salles de bain en marbre, les bougies flottantes et les effets architecturaux attestent de l'amour du détail.

Las exóticas bellezas en el baño de mármol, las velas flotantes y los efectos arquitectónicos son una prueba del gusto por el detalle.

Bellezze esotiche nella stanza da bagno di marmo, candele galleggianti ed effetti architettonici dimostrano l'amore per il dettaglio.

Paintings by local artists and precious items from Africa and Asia enchant the facility's suites and restaurants.

Gemälde lokaler Künstler und Preziosen aus Afrika und Asien verzaubern die Suiten und Restaurants der Anlage.

Des peintures d'artistes locaux et des précieuses originaires d'Afrique et d'Asie agrémentent les suites et le restaurant du domaine.

Las pinturas de los artistas locales y las alhajas procedentes de África y Asia proporcionan un toque mágico a las suites y los restaurantes del complejo.

I quadri di pittori locali ed oggetti preziosi dall'Africa e l'Asia incantano le suites ed i ristoranti dell'impianto.

The Leela Goa

Goa, India

The decorative facades shine pink like a blooming Bougainvillea—the beauty of the palace architecture from the 13th century was given a modern interpretation here. The guests experience a successful symbiosis of Portuguese and Indian design elements in the suites. In some of the suites, exquisite antiques are reminiscent of India's glamorous past. From all rooms, one can overlook the romantic lagoons and a pool with a waterfall in the midst of an exotic garden.

Rosa wie blühende Bougainvillea leuchten die dekorativen Fassaden der Bungalows – die Schönheit der Palastarchitektur aus dem 13. Jahrhundert wurde hier modern interpretiert. In den Suiten erleben die Gäste eine gelungene Symbiose von portugiesischen und indischen Designelementen. In einigen der Suiten erinnern ausgesuchte Antiquitäten an die glanzvolle Vergangenheit Indiens. Von allen Zimmern aus überblickt man romantische Lagunen und einen Pool mit Wasserfall inmitten exotischer Gärten.

Les façades décoratives des bungalows – une interprétation moderne de la beauté de l'architecture des palais du 13ième siècle – sont roses comme des bougainvilliers en fleur. Dans les suites, l'hôte peut admirer une symbiose réussie d'éléments ornamentaux portugais et indiens. Dans certaines suites, des antiquités choisies rappellent le passé glorieux de l'Inde. De toutes les chambres, on peut admirer la lagune romantique et un bassin situé au milieu d'un jardin exotique et arrosé par une cascade.

De color de rosa como las buganvillas en flor lucen las decorativas fachadas de los bungalows –la belleza de la arquitectura palaciega del siglo XIII se ofrece aquí en una interpretación moderna. En las suites los huéspedes experimentan una acertada simbiosis entre elementos de diseño portugueses e indios. En algunas de las suites las antigüedades escogidas recuerdan el esplendoroso pasado de la India. Desde todas las habitaciones se pueden contemplar románticas lagunas y una piscina con cascada rodeada de exóticos jardines.

Le facciate decorate dei bungalows brillano di colore rosa come una bougainvillea fiorita – la bellezza dell'architettura dei palazzi del trecento è stata riinterpretata in modo moderno. Nelle suites gli ospiti vivono l'esperienza di una riuscita simbiosi tra elementi del design portughese ed indiano. In alcune suites antichità selezionate ricordano il glorioso passato dell'India. Da tutte le camere ci si può godere il panorama su romantiche lagune ed una piscina con una cascata in mezzo a giardini esotici.

The palm tree beach stretches out for miles in front of the resort. Shady terraces, pool landscapes, and lagoons pass right through the premises.

Meilenweit erstreckt sich der Palmenstrand vor dem Resort. Schattige Terrassen, Pool-Landschaften und Lagunen durchziehen das Gelände.

La plage de palmiers s'étend sur des kilomètres devant le domaine. Des terrasses ombragées, des paysages de bassins et de lagunes traversent le domaine.

La playa flanqueada de palmeras se extiende a lo largo de varias millas ante el complejo. El recinto está surcado de terrazas sombrías, piscinas y lagunas.

Per miglia la spiaggia di palme si estende davanti al resort. Terrazze ombreggiate, paesaggi di piscine e lagune percorrono la tenuta.

Over the bungalows of the new Leela Club with pink colored walls and elegant suites, the fat-bellied elephant-god Ganesh keeps an eye on things.

Über die Bungalows des neuen Leela Clubs mit den pinkfarbenen Mauern und eleganten Suiten wacht der dickbäuchige Elefantengott Ganesh.

Sur les bungalows du nouveau Leela Club aux murs de couleur rose fuchsia et aux suites élégantes veille le dieu des éléphants au gros ventre, Ganesh.

Los bungalows del nuevo Leela Club con sus muros color de rosa y sus elegantes suites son vigilados por el barrigudo Dios Elefante Ganesh.

Il panciuto dio Ganesh sorveglia le villette del nuovo Leela Club con i suoi muri di colore rosa e le eleganti suites.

Four Seasons Resort Maldives at Kuda Huraa

Kuda Huraa, Maldives

The highlight on Kuda Huraa in the northern Malé atoll is the small, white sand-hemmed spa island in the midst of crystal clear, turquoise glimmering water, which one reaches with the Dhoni, a traditional wooden boat. The 106 guest pavilions are spread out over a five-hectare estate. The water bungalows, built on stilts, are most spectacular and their partially room-high glazed panes impart the feeling of being one with the sea.

Highlight auf Kuda Huraa im nördlichen Malé-Atoll ist die kleine, von blendend weißem Sand umsäumte Spa-Insel inmitten glasklaren, türkisblau schimmernden Wassers, die man mit dem Dhoni, dem traditionellen Holzboot, erreicht. Die 106 Gästepavillons verteilen sich über ein fünf Hektar großes Gelände. Am spektakulärsten sind die auf Stelzen gebauten Wasserbungalows, die mit ihren teilweise raumhoch verglasten Scheiben das Gefühl vermitteln, eins mit dem Meer zu sein.

L'île spa au sable fin d'une blancheur éblouissante et entourée d'une eau claire de couleur turquoise que l'on ne peut atteindre qu'avec le Dhoni, la barque traditionnelle, est attraction sur Kuda Huraa, dans l'atoll de Malé, au Nord des Maldives. Les 106 pavillons d'hôtes sont dispersés sur les cinq hectares du domaines. Les plus spectaculaires sont les bungalows sur pilotis qui grâce à leurs murs vitrés hauts parfois comme le bâtiment donnent l'impression de faire corps avec la mer.

La pequeña isla de Spa, rodeada de arena deslumbrantemente blanca en medio de un agua cristalina de reflejos turquesas, a la que se llega embarcado en un Dhoni, la embarcación de madera tradicional, es la atracción más destacada en Kuda Huraa, al norte del atolón de Malé. Los 106 pabellones para huéspedes están distribuidos en un recinto de cinco hectáreas. Los más espectaculares son los bungalows acuáticos construidos sobre pilones de madera, que con sus ventanales que en parte alcanzan el techo dan la sensación de estar formando parte del mar.

Il clou su Kuda Huraa nell'atollo settentrionale di Malé è rappresentato da una piccola isola spa contornata di una spiaggia di sabbia bianca splendente, in mezzo all'acqua limpida turchese. L'isola si raggiunge con un dhoni, la tradizionale barca di legno. I 106 padiglioni per gli ospiti si distribuiscono su un terreno di cinque ettari. Le villette costruite su pali nell'acqua sono le più spettacolari e con le loro vetrate che in parte coprono tutta la parete, danno l'impressione di formare un'unità con il mare.

In the spa pavilions built on stilts in the sea, relaxing treatments are administered, for instance a Maldivian Monsoon Ritual.

In den auf Stelzen ins Meer gebauten Spa-Pavillons werden entspannende Behandlungen verabreicht, zum Beispiel ein Maledivian Monsoon Ritual.

Dans les pavillons spa construits sur pilotis, des traitements relaxants sont proposés, tels que le rituel maldivien monsoon.

En los pabellones Spa construidos sobre pilones en el mar se administran tratamientos relajantes como, por ejemplo, un ritual del monzón de las Maldivas.

Nei padiglioni spa costruiti su pali nel mare si effettuano trattamenti rilassanti, come ad esempio il rituale del Maledivian Monsoon.

The guest receives the natural ingredients before each treatment, wonderfully arranged, served on a tray.

Vor jeder Behandlung bekommt der Gast die natürlichen Ingredienzien, wunderbar arrangiert, auf einem Tablett präsentiert.

Avant chaque traitement, les ingrédients naturels sont présentés à l'hôte avec faste sur un plateau.

Antes de cada tratamiento al huésped se le presentan los ingredientes preparados cuidadosamente sobre una bandeja.

Prima di ogni trattamento, all'ospite vengono presentati gli ingredienti naturali, arrangiati in modo meraviglioso su un vassoio.

Cocoa Island

Makunufushi, Maldives

Small wooden huts contain the accommodations standing directly in the ocean on posts and accessible by footbridges. Each has its own small terrace, from which a couple of stairs lead down to the water. The luxury suites are designed with two floors—the living area on the lower and a separate sleeping area on the upper level. Their unusually simple furnishings remind one of the traditional Maldivian boats.

Kleine Holzhütten enthalten die Unterkünfte, die auf Pfählen direkt im Meer stehen und über Stege zu erreichen sind. Jede hat eine eigene kleine Terrasse, von der ein paar Treppenstufen hinab ins Wasser führen. Die Luxussuiten sind zweistöckig angelegt – mit Wohnbereich auf der unteren und einem separaten Schlafbereich auf der oberen Ebene. Ihre ungewöhnlich schlichte Ausstattung soll an traditionelle maledivische Boote erinnern.

Les logements se trouvent dans de petites cabanes en bois situées directement sur la mer grâce à leurs pilotis et que l'on peut atteindre par des passerelles. Chacun a sa terrasse éloignée de l'eau que de quelques marches. Les suites de luxe sont construites sur deux étages – un espace de vie à l'étage inférieur et un espace pour dormir séparé à l'étage supérieur. Leur aménagement extrêmement sobre est là pour rappeler les bateaux maldiviens traditionnels.

Los alojamientos se encuentran en pequeñas cabañas de madera construidas sobre pilones, en el mar, a las que se llega cruzando puentecillos. Cada una tiene su propia pequeña terraza desde la que unos pocos escalones conducen al agua. Las suites de lujo son dúplex, con la zona de estar en el piso inferior y la zona separada de los dormitorios en el superior. El equipamiento extraordinariamente evoca las embarcaciones típicas maldivas.

Piccole capanne di legno contengono gli alloggi che sono stati costruiti su pali direttamente nel mare e raggiungibili attraverso passerelle di legno. Ognuna ha una piccola terrazza che porta all'acqua, scendendo qualche scalino. Le suites di lusso sono state costruite su due piani – con la zona soggiorno al piano inferiore e la zona riposo al piano superiore. L'arredamento inconsuetamente semplice vuole ricordare le tradizionali barche maldive.

Living in the middle of the ocean: the pile-dwellings of Cocoa Island are very modern inside, furnished nearly minimalist.

Wohnen mitten im Meer: Die Pfahlbauten von Cocoa Island sind im Inneren sehr modern, beinahe minimalistisch eingerichtet.

Habiter au milieu de la mer : les bâtiments sur pilotis de l'île Cocoa sont très modernes à l'intérieur, aménagés de façon presque minimaliste.

Vivir en medio del mar: Los palafitos de la Isla Cocoa tienen un equipamiento muy moderno, casi minimalista.

Abitare in mezzo al mare: le costruzioni a pali di Cocoa Island sono state arredate in modo molto moderno, quasi minimalistico.

The elegant, unobtrusive furnishings don't sidetrack from the view of the ocean and on up to the horizon.

Die elegante, zurückhaltende Einrichtung lenkt nicht vom Meeresblick bis zum Horizont ab.

L'aménagement élégant et discret ne perturbe pas la vue allant de la mer à l'horizon.

El mobiliario elegante y discreto no distrae de la vista al mar que se extiende hasta el horizonte.

L'arredamento elegante e discreto non distoglie dalla vista sul mare fino all'orizzonte.

Cocoa Island *Makunufushi, Maldives*   109

In an open hut, an extensive offering of yoga courses and wellness awaits the guest.

In offenen Hütten erwartet den Gast ein umfangreiches Angebot an Yogakursen und Wellness.

Dans les cabanes ouvertes, une offre complète de cours de yoga et de bien-être attend l'hôte.

En las cabañas abiertas al huésped le espera una amplia oferta de cursos de yoga y wellness.

Nelle capanne aperte l'ospite riceve una vasta offerta di corsi di yoga e wellness.

Taj Exotica Resort & Spa

Malé Atoll, Maldives

Pure nature awaits the visitor: the varied buildings were erected with the least possible intervention in the surroundings and consist largely of natural materials—from wooden floors to the palm-frond covered roof. The guest can look over the Indian Ocean already from bed, regardless of whether an accommodation on the beach or one of the pile dwellings on the water was chosen. The interior rooms are designed quite simple; yet they offer the comfort of a luxury hotel.

Natur pur erwartet den Besucher: Die verschiedenen Gebäude wurden mit kleinstmöglichem Eingriff in die Umgebung errichtet und bestehen weitgehend aus natürlichen Materialen – vom Holzboden bis zum palmwedelgedeckten Dach. Bereits vom Bett aus kann der Gast über den Indischen Ozean schauen, egal ob er eine Unterkunft am Strand oder einen der Pfahlbauten im Wasser gewählt hat. Die Innenräume sind recht einfach gestaltet, dennoch bieten sie den Komfort eines Luxushotels.

La nature pure attend le visiteur : Les différents bâtiments ont été construits dans le respect de leur environnement et le plus possible avec des matériaux naturels – des sols en bois jusqu'au toit recouvert de palmes. De son lit, l'hôte peut admirer l'océan Indien, qu'il ait choisit un logement près de la plage ou un logement sur pilotis. Les espaces intérieurs ont été aménagés avec simplicité mais offrent le confort d'un hôtel de luxe.

La naturaleza en estado puro espera al visitante. Las distintas edificaciones han sido construidas con la menor agresión posible hacia el entorno y están hechas en su mayoría de materiales naturales, desde el suelo de madera hasta el techo cubierto de hojas de palma. Desde su propia cama el huésped puede contemplar el Océano Índico, tanto si ha escogido un alojamiento en la playa como uno de los palafitos en el agua. Las estancias interiores tienen un equipamiento sencillo, aunque no obstante ofrecen el confort de un hotel de lujo.

La pura natura aspetta l'ospite. I vari edifici sono stati costruiti intervenendo meno possibile sui dintorni e consistono prevalentemente di materiali naturali – dal pavimento di legno fino al tetto ricoperto di rami di palme. Già dal letto l'ospite può osservare l'Oceano Indiano, indipendentemente dalla scelta di un alloggio sulla spiaggia o in una delle costruzioni su pali nell'acqua. I vani interni sono stati creati in modo relativamente semplice; ciononostante offrono il confort di un hotel di lusso.

Dark wood, pastel colors and cream hues characterize the rooms.

Dunkles Holz, Pastellfarben und Cremetöne bestimmen die Räume.

Du bois sombre, des couleurs pastel et des tons crème caractérisent les espaces.

Los espacios se caracterizan por la madera oscura, los colores pastel y las tonalidades crema.

Il legno scuro, i colori pastelli e la tonalità di crema caratterizzano i vani.

Not an exaggerated ostentatious furnishing, but the unique view is what forms the luxury of the hotel.

Nicht eine übertrieben prunkvolle Ausstattung, sondern die einmalige Aussicht macht den Luxus des Hotels aus.

Le luxe de cet hôtel ne réside pas dans un aménagement somptueux mais dans la beauté de la vue imprenable.

El lujo del hotel está determinado por la inmejorable vista, no por la decoración excesivamente suntuosa.

Non è un arredamento eccessivamente sontuoso, ma è l'eccezionale panorama che rappresenta il lusso dell'hotel.

Hilton Maldives

Rangali Island, Maldives

The individual resort villas are distributed on two small islands, connected with each other via a footbridge. In the spa area—erected like part of the villas in the ocean—a glass surface is set into the floor, offering the guest a special kind of view: the guest can look out onto the water and watch how the fish swim through under the building. The villas made from Canadian cedar wood and with a view of the Indian Ocean are furnished with four-poster beds.

Die einzelnen Villen des Resorts verteilen sich auf zwei kleine Inseln, die über einen Steg miteinander verbunden sind. Im Spa-Bereich – ebenso wie ein Teil der Villen im Meer errichtet – ist eine Glasfläche in den Boden eingelassen, die dem Gast eine Aussicht der besonderen Art bietet: Er kann aufs Wasser schauen und beobachten, wie die Fische unter dem Gebäude hindurch schwimmen. Die Villen aus kanadischem Zedernholz und mit Blick auf den Indischen Ozean sind mit Himmelbetten ausgestattet.

Les différentes villas du domaine sont dispersées sur deux petites îles, reliées entre elles par une passerelle. Dans le domaine spa – comme dans une partie des villas qui se trouvent sur la mer – il y une surface vitrée encastrée dans le sol qui offre à l'hôte un spectacle tout particulier : celui-ci peut regarder dans l'eau et observer les poissons nageant sous le bâtiment. Les villas en bois de cèdre du Canada et dotées d'une vue imprenable sur l'océan Indien possèdent des lits à baldaquin.

Los chalés individuales del complejo se reparten en dos pequeñas islas unidas entre sí por una pasarela. En la zona de Spa, construida sobre el mar, igual que una parte de los chalés, se ha incluido una superficie de cristal en el suelo que ofrece al huésped una vista muy especial. Puede contemplar el agua y observar cómo los peces nadan por debajo de la cabaña. Los chalés de madera de cedro canadiense con vista al Océano Índico están provistas de camas con dosel.

Le singole ville del resort si distribuiscono su due piccole isole che sono collegate tra loro con una passerella di legno. Nell'area spa che è stata eretta in mezzo al mare così come una parte delle ville, è stata inserita nel pavimento una superficie di vetro che offre una vista del tutto particolare all'ospite. Egli può vedere l'acqua sottostante, osservando i pesci nuotanti sotto l'edificio. Le ville di legno di cedro canadese che danno il panorama sull'Oceano Indiano, sono provvisti di letti a baldacchino.

Whoever takes his quarters in this hotel must not be water-shy. This element surrounds the guests, regardless where they look.

Wer sein Quartier in diesem Hotel bezieht, darf nicht wasserscheu sein. Dieses Element umgibt den Gast, egal wohin er schaut.

Les clients de cet hôtel qui choisissent de dormir ici ne doivent pas craindre l'eau. Cet élément entoure l'hôte partout où on se trouve.

Aquél que escoja este hotel como alojamiento no debe tenerle miedo al agua. Este elemento rodea al huésped por todas partes.

Chi s'accinge ad alloggiare in questo hotel non deve temere l'acqua. L'ospite è circondato da quest'elemento, ovunque lo sguardo vaghi.

Modern comfort *inside and archaic hut-aesthetic outside.*

Moderner Komfort *innen und archaische Hüttenästhetik außen.*

Confort moderne *à l'intérieur et esthétique archaïque des cabanes à l'extérieur.*

Moderno confort *por dentro y arcaica estética de cabaña por fuera.*

Confort moderno *all'interno ed estetica di capanne arcaiche all'esterno.*

Amankila

Bali, Indonesia

Translated, "Amankila" means something like "peaceful hill". A glance down the Bali coastal cliffs takes in a striking ensemble of a tiered pool system. But it is not only the typical thatched roofs that authentically reflect the national culture. The entire resort would be reminiscent of a monastic way of life were it not for the great comfort of the 34 freestanding suites.

Übersetzt heißt „Amankila" soviel wie „friedlicher Hügel". Der Blick abwärts der balinesischen Küstenklippen umfasst ein imposantes Ensemble eines gestuften Poolsystems. Doch sind es nicht allein die typischen strohgedeckten Dächer, die hier die Landeskultur auf authentische Weise widerspiegeln. Das gesamte Resort erinnerte an eine klösterliche Lebenswelt, wäre da nicht der ganze Komfort der 34 jeweils freistehenden Suiten.

« Amankila » signifie « la colline de la paix ». Lorsque le regard se plonge sur les falaises de Bali, il embrasse un ensemble imposant de bassins d'eau disposés en cascade. Cependant, les toits de pailles ne sont pas les seuls à représenter de façon authentique la culture locale. Le domaine entier rappellerait une vie au couvent, s'il n'offrait pas dans les 34 suites indépendantes le confort complet.

"Amankila" quiere decir algo así como "colina pacífica". La vista sobre los acantilados balineses abarca el imponente conjunto de un sistema de piscinas escalonadas. No son sólo los típicos tejados cubiertos de paja los que reflejan de manera auténtica la cultura regional. Todo el complejo recordaría una forma de vida monástica de no existir el confort completo de las 34 suites distribuidas de manera aislada.

Tradotto "Amankila" significa tanto quanto "collina pacifica". Lo sguarda in giù, verso gli scogli della costa balinese raccoglie un insieme imponente di un sistema di piscine a terrazze. Però non sono soltanto i tetti tradizionali ricoperti di paglia che rispecchiano la cultura del paese in modo autentico. Tutto il resort ricorderebbe il mondo dei monasteri, se non fosse per il confort delle 34 suites indipendenti.

Amankila has been inviting one to discover and enjoy Balinese culture in an exposed location already since 1992.

Bereits seit 1992 lädt Amankila dazu ein, balinesische Kultur in exponierter Lage zu entdecken und zu genießen.

Depuis déjà 1992, Amankila invite à découvrir et à goûter la culture balinaise dans un environnement privilégié.

Ya desde 1992 Amankila invita a descubrir y disfrutar de la cultura balinesa desde un lugar privilegiado.

Già dal 1992 l'Amankila invita a scoprire e godersi la cultura balinese in una posizione esposta.

Strolling and Buddhist contemplativeness in open architecture. Also for lovers of the written word.

Lustwandeln und buddhistische Beschaulichkeit in offener Architektur. Auch für Freunde des geschriebenen Wortes.

Déambulation et sérénité bouddhique dans une architecture ouverte. Destinée aussi aux amis du livre.

Paseo y contemplación budista en una arquitectura abierta. También para los amigos de la palabra escrita.

Passeggiate e tranquillità buddista in un'architettura aperta. Pure per gli amici della parola scritta.

Four Seasons Resort Bali at Jimbaran Bay

Bali, Indonesia

Embedded in a rambling tropical garden landscape in the south of Bali on the Bukit peninsula sits the resort that was one of the first to offer private villas with small pools rather than rooms. One has a perfect view of the Jimbaran Bay beach from each of the 147 sanctuaries. The thatched roof pavilions of at least 200-m² living space were built in traditional Balinese style with Salas, as the open, light-flooded living areas are called.

Eingebettet in eine weitläufige tropische Gartenlandschaft im Süden Balis auf der Halbinsel Bukit liegt das Resort, das als eines der ersten statt Zimmern Privatvillen mit kleinen Pools anbot. Von jedem dieser 147 Refugien hat man einen Traumblick auf den Strand der Jimbaran Bay. Die reetgedeckten Pavillons mit mindestens 200 m² Wohnfläche wurden im traditionellen balinesischen Stil erbaut, mit Salas, wie die offenen lichtdurchfluteten Wohnräume genannt werden.

Le domaine est plongé dans un paysage étendu de jardin tropical, au Sud de Bali, sur la presqu'île de Bukit ; il était un des premiers à offrir des villas privées avec piscine au lieu de chambres. Depuis ses 147 refuges, on a une vue de rêve sur la plage du Jimbaran. Les pavillons au toit de chaume d'une surface d'au moins 200 m² d'espace habitable ont été construits dans le style traditionnel balinais, avec des salas, conformément au nom que l'on donne aux espaces habitables ouverts baignés de lumière.

Intercalado en un extenso paisaje ajardinado tropical en el sur de Bali en la península de Bukit se halla este complejo que fue de los primeros en ofrecer en lugar de habitaciones chalés privados con pequeñas piscinas. Desde cada uno de estos 147 refugios se tiene una vista de ensueño de la playa de la bahía de Jimbaran. Los pabellones cubiertos de caña con un mínimo de 200 m² de superficie habitable fueron construidos al estilo tradicional balinés, con "salas", como son llamadas las estancias abiertas inundadas de luz.

Inserito in un vasto paesaggio di giardini esotici nel Sud di Bali sulla peninsola di Bukit si trova il resort che è stato tra i primi ad offrire ville private con una piccola piscina al posto di camere. Da ognuno di questi 147 rifugi si ha un panorama da sogno sulla spiaggia di Jimbaran Bay. I padiglioni ricoperti di canne con una superficie di almeno 200 m² sono stati costruiti nello stile tradizionale balinese, con salas, come si suol chiamare i locali da soggiorno ampi e luminosi.

The Jimbaran bay with the three-kilometer fine-grained sand beach.

Die Jimbaran-Bucht mit dem drei Kilometer langen feinkörnigen Sandstrand.

La baie de Jimbaran avec sa plage de sable extra fin de trois kilomètres.

La bahía de Jimbaran con su playa de arena fina de tres kilómetros de longitud.

La baia di Jimbaran con la spiaggia di sabbia fine lunga tre chilometri.

Each guest pavilion *has a Sala fitted with Balinese furniture and a 12-m² private pool.*

Jeder Gästepavillon *hat eine mit balinesischen Möbeln eingerichtete Sala und einen 12 m² großen Privatpool.*

Chaque pavillon *possède une sala aménagée avec des meubles balinais et une piscine privée de 12 m².*

Cada pabellón de huéspedes *tiene una "sala" amueblada al estilo balinés y una piscina privada de 12 m².*

Ogni padiglione degli ospiti *ha una sala arredata con mobili balinesi ed una piscina privata con una superficie di 12 m².*

The Legian &
Club at The Legian

Bali, Indonesia

As it was originally planned as an apartment block the accommodation in this hotel offers lots of space. Its 67 suits offer particularly generous measurements, 14 apartments have two bedrooms and an area of 150 m²—ideal for families or small groups. The newly opened "Club at the Legian" additionally offers ten private villas. The fittings are regionally inspired: parquet flooring made of Balinese mahogany, textiles woven by local craftsmen and statutes carved by Indonesian artists.

Viel Raum bieten die Unterkünfte dieses Hotels, denn es war ursprünglich als Apartmentanlage geplant. Daher sind seine 67 Suiten besonders großzügig bemessen; alleine 14 davon haben zwei Schlafzimmer und eine Fläche von 150 m² – ideal für Familien oder Kleingruppen. Der neu eröffnete „Club at the Legian" wartet zusätzlich mit zehn privaten Villen auf. Die Ausstattung setzt auf Regionales: Parkett aus balinesischem Mahagoni, Stoffe, die von einheimischen Handwerkern gewebt wurden, und Statuen von indonesischen Künstlern.

Les logements de cet hôtel offrent beaucoup d'espace car ils étaient autrefois destinés à être des appartements. C'est ce qui explique que ses 67 suites aient des tailles particulièrement généreuses; 14 d'entre elles ont deux chambres à coucher et une surface de 150 m² – idéal pour une famille ou un petit groupe. Le « Club at the Legian », nouvellement inauguré, offre dix villas privées supplémentaires. L'aménagement est en style régional : parquets en acajou balinais, des étoffes tissées par des artisans locaux et des statues réalisées par des artistes indonésiens.

Los alojamientos de este hotel ofrecen mucho espacio, ya que inicialmente fue concebido como un complejo de viviendas. Por esta razón, sus 67 suites son especialmente amplias. 14 de ellas tienen dos dormitorios y una superficie de 150 m² –ideal para familias o grupos pequeños. El "Club at the Legian", nuevamente inaugurado, presenta diez chalés privados adicionales. La decoración se basa en lo regional: Parquet de caoba balinesa, tejidos de artesanos locales, y estatuas de artistas indonesios.

Gli alloggi di questo hotel offrono molto spazio perché originariamente era previsto come impianto residence. Per questo motivo le 67 suites sono di dimensioni particolarmente generose; 14 di esse dispongono di due camere da letto ed una superficie di 150 m² – l'ideale per famiglie o piccoli gruppi. Il "Club at the Legian" appena aperto offre altre dieci ville private. L'arredamento punta sul regionale: palquet di mogano balinese, stoffe tessute da artigiani locali e statue d'artisti indonesi.

The tower with the stairs is a tribute to the Balinese sacral architecture: the inhabitants of the villages were called to prayer from the traditional Kulkul towers.

Der Treppenturm ist eine Hommage an die balinesische Sakralarchitektur: Von den traditionellen Kulkul-Türmen wurden die Dorfbewohner zum Tempel gerufen.

La tour en escalier est un hommage à l'architecture sacrale balinaise : Des tours traditionnelles kulkul, les habitants du village étaient invités à se rendre au temple.

La torre de la escalera es un homenaje a la arquitectura sacra balinesa. Desde las tradicionales torres Kulkul eran llamados al templo los habitantes de la aldea.

La torre a scale rappresenta un hommage all'architettura sacrale balinese. Dalle tradizionali torri kulkul gli abitanti dei paesi venivano chiamati al tempio.

A mixture of modern architecture and traditional forms gives the hotel its characteristic flair.

Ein Mix aus moderner Architektur und traditionellen Formen prägt das Hotel.

L'hôtel est caractérisé par un mélange d'architecture moderne et des formes traditionnelles.

El hotel se caracteriza por una combinación de arquitectura moderna con formas tradicionales.

Un misto tra architettura moderna e forme tradizionali caratterizza l'hotel.

Amanpuri
Phuket, Thailand

Stirring up the joy of experiencing foreign cultures combined with the desire to pamper and a sense for the unusual—that constitutes the philosophy of all Aman resorts. Amanpuri belongs to this squad of exceptional destinations. Situated in the environs of a former coconut plantation, the facility unites Buddhist grace with stylistic focus on essentials and thus creates an ambience of western generosity—a view of the tropical beach life and a diamond-clear ocean included.

Die Freude am Erleben fremder Kulturen wecken, vereint mit der Lust zum Verwöhnen und dem Sinn für das Außergewöhnliche – das macht die Philosophie aller Aman-Resorts aus. Amanpuri gehört mit in die Riege dieser ausgefallenen Reiseziele. In der Umgebung einer ehemaligen Kokosnussplantage gelegen, vereint die Anlage buddhistische Anmut mit stilistischer Konzentration auf das Wesentliche und schafft so ein Ambiente von westlicher Großzügigkeit – den Blick auf tropisches Strandleben und ein diamantklares Meer eingeschlossen.

Le plaisir de découvrir une culture étrangère associé à l'envie de combler ses clients et au goût pour l'extraordinaire – voilà comment résumer la philosophie de tous les domaines Aman. Amanpuri appartient à cette série de destinations touristiques insolites. Il est situé à proximité d'un ancien plantage de noix de coco et réunit l'élégance bouddhique à une concentration stylistique pour l'essentiel et créé ainsi une ambiance de générosité occidentale – la vue sur la vie balnéaire tropicale et sur une mer claire comme du diamant inclus.

La filosofía de todos los resorts Aman es despertar la alegría de conocer culturas extranjeras, unida al placer del trato exquisito y a la sensibilidad por lo excepcional. Amanpuri también figura en la lista de estos destinos especiales. Ubicado en las inmediaciones de una antigua plantación de coco, este resort combina el encanto budista con un estilo basado en lo esencial, logrando de este modo un ambiente de amplitud occidental –incluyendo la vista a una playa tropical y un mar de claridad diamantina.

Risvegliare la gioia di sperimentare altre culture, unita alla voglia di farsi viziare ed il senso per lo straordinario – è questa la filosofia dell'Aman Resort. Amanpuri fa parte di queste mete di viaggio inconsuete. L'impianto si trova nei dintorni di una piantagione di una volta di noci di cocco e riunisce la grazia buddista con la concentrazione stilistica sull'essenziale, creando così un ambiente di generosità dell'Ovest – inclusa la vista sulla vita di spiaggia ed un mare limpido come un diamante.

Clear forms and peaceful moments set the tone of the Amanpuri design.

Klare Formen und stille Momente bestimmen das Design von Amanpuri.

Des formes simples et des espaces de repos sont caractéristiques du design d'Amanpuri.

Formas claras y factores de tranquilidad determinan el diseño de Amanpuri.

Forme chiare e momenti di tranquillità determinano il design d'Amanpuri.

Only a few steps from the beach on the one hand, shady spots on the other—a resort that knows how to arrange idyll.

Nur wenige Schritte zum Strand auf der einen Seite, schattenspendende Plätze auf der anderen – ein Resort, das Idylle zu gestalten weiß.

A quelques pas de la plage, des places ombrageuses d'un côté et de l'autre – un domaine qui sait comment se fabrique l'idyllique.

A pocos pasos de la playa, por una parte, y con lugares umbríos, por otra – un resort que sabe dar forma a lo idílico.

A soli pochi passi dalla spiaggia da una parte, e posti ombreggiati dall'altra – un resort che sa creare l'idillico.

Banyan Tree Phuket

Phuket, Thailand

The repeatedly awarded resort offers an exclusive ensemble of spacious villas grouped around their pools. Gardens with lotus ponds and meditation rooms—all in the Siamese exalted-classical style—line the individually and openly designed rooms. A thoroughly intimate setting—even on the stretching hotel beach.

Das mehrfach ausgezeichnete Resort bietet ein exklusives Ensemble von geräumigen Villen, die sich um die zugehörigen Pools gruppieren. Gärten mit Lotusteichen und Meditationsräume – alles im gehoben-klassischen Stil der Siamesen – säumen die individuell und offen gestalteten Räumlichkeiten. Eine durch und durch intime Inszenierung – auch am sich dahinstreckenden Strand des Hauses.

Le domaine, plusieurs fois primé, offre un ensemble exclusif de vastes villas regroupées autour de leurs piscines. Des jardins contenant des bassins de lotus et des espaces de médiation – le tout dans le style classique et raffiné des siamois – entourent les espaces individuels, à l'architecture ouverte. Une mise en scène des plus intimes – et cela jusqu'à la plage s'étendant aux pieds de la maison.

Este resort, galardonado en reiteradas ocasiones, ofrece un conjunto exclusivo de amplios chalés que se agrupan alrededor de las respectivas piscinas. Los jardines con pequeños estanques de lotos y salas de meditación –todo ello en un elegante estilo clásico siamés– bordean las habitaciones de diseño individual y abierto: Un escenario absolutamente íntimo –también en la playa que se extiende a lo largo del resort.

Il resort premiato ripetutamente offre un insieme esclusivo di ville spaziose che si raggruppano attorno alle loro piscine. I giardini con stagni coperti di fiori di loto e stanze per la meditazione – il tutto nello stile classico-superiore dei siamesi – contornano i vani disegnati in modo individuale ed aperto. Una messa in scena del tutto intima – anche per quanto riguarda la lunga spiaggia dell'hotel.

Every door in Banyan Tree opens onto multifaceted views of Thai culture and hospitality.

Mit jeder Tür im Banyan Tree öffnen sich vielfältige Aussichten auf die thailändische Kultur und Gastfreundschaft.

Au Banyan Tree, chaque porte ouverte permet de découvrir une nouvelle facette de la culture thaïlandaise et de son hospitalité.

Con cada puerta en el Banyan Tree se abren numerosas posibilidades para conocer la cultura y la hospitalidad tailandesa.

Con ogni porta del Banyan Tree si offrono vedute sfaccettate sulla cultura ed ospitalità tailandese.

Lost steps *on the beach—symbol of a spot where every villa offers a very intimate spot combined with the stimulus of an exotic culture and spiritual world.*

Verlorene Schritte *am Strand – Sinnbild für einen Ort, an dem jede Villa einen ganz intimen Platz bietet, verbunden mit dem Reiz einer exotischen Kultur und Geisteswelt.*

Des pas perdus *sur la plage – une image pleine de sens pour un lieu où chaque villa offre un espace très intime; le tout associé à la découverte d'une culture exotique et de son environnement spirituel.*

Pasos perdidos *en la playa –símbolo de un lugar, en el que cada chalé ofrece un espacio íntimo, unido al atractivo de una cultura y un mundo espiritual exóticos.*

Passi persi *sulla spiaggia – simbolo per un luogo ove ogni villa offre uno spazio tutto privato, insieme all'attrattività di una cultura ed un mondo intellettuale esotico.*

JW Marriot Phuket Resort and Spa

Phuket, Thailand

The Marriott resort opens up a universe of its own. No wonder in a hotel that, due to its size, offers all possible amenities. Children play in their own "Little Turtle Pool". From the king-size bed in the suites, the cool water nearly lays at ones feet. Moreover, architecture and decoration impart an original "touch of Thailand". Spa, palm garden and hotel beach take care of the rest. A dreamlike set—latest at night when a flickering sea of lights surrounds the facility.

Das Marriott-Resort öffnet den Zugang zu einem eigenen Universum. Kein Wunder bei einem Haus, das dank seiner Größe alle erdenklichen Annehmlichkeiten bietet. Die Kinder vergnügen sich im eigenen Little Turtle Pool. Den Großen liegt vom King Size-Bett der Suiten aus das kühle Nass fast zu Füßen. Architektur und Dekorationen vermitteln dazu einen originären „touch of Thailand". Spa, Palmengarten und Hotelstrand tun ihr Übriges. Eine traumähnliche Kulisse – spätestens zur Nacht, wenn die Anlage ein flackerndes Lichtermeer umhüllt.

Le domaine Marriott est une invitation dans un univers à part entière. Ce n'est pas étonnant pour une maison dont la taille permet d'offrir toutes les commodités imaginables. Les enfants s'amusent dans la piscine aux tortues, Little Turtle Pool. L'eau rafraîchissante se arrive presque aux pieds des plus grands depuis le lit grande taille des suites. L'architecture et la décoration communiquent une touche originale « très thaïlandaise ». Le spa, la palmeraie et la plage de l'hôtel font le reste. Une coulisse de rêve – au plus tard, dans la nuit, lorsque le domaine est entouré par une mer de lumières chatoyantes.

Sin duda alguna, el Marriot Resort permite acceder a un universo propio. Esto no es sorprendente en un hotel que gracias a su extensión puede ofrecer todas las comodidades imaginables. Los niños pueden disfrutar de su propia Little Turtle Pool y los adultos tienen el agua refrescante casi al pie de sus camas king size en las suites. La arquitectura y la decoración proporcionan un auténtico "touch of Thailand". El Spa, el jardín de palmas y la playa del hotel hacen el resto. Un escenario de ensueño –a más tardar por la noche, cuando el resort se envuelve en un llameante mar de luces.

Indubbiamente il Marriott-Resort apre la porta ad un universo proprio. Ciò non stupisce, visto che l'hotel grazie alla sua dimensione offre tutti i confort pensabili. I bambini si divertono nel Little Turtle Pool riservato a loro. Per i grandi la frescura dell'acqua si trova in pratica ai piedi scendendo dal letto king size. L'architettura e le decorazioni ci aggiungono l'originale "touch of Thailand". Lo spa, il giardino di palme e la spiaggia dell'hotel contribuiscono la loro parte. Un fondo da sogno – al più tardi di notte quando la tenuta è sommersa in un mare di luci da fiaccole.

*A **mirror** of Balinese advanced civilization. The design of the hotel and its decoration are picturesque and Daedalian but still concentrated.*

*Ein **Spiegel** der balinesischen Hochkultur. Das Design des Hauses und seine Dekorationen sind bild- und blumenreich und doch konzentriert.*

*Un **miroir** de la culture balinaise. Le design de la maison et ses décorations contiennent une profusion d'images et de fleurs et sont pourtant très concentrées.*

*Un **reflejo** de la civilización balinesa. En el diseño y decoración del hotel abundan los cuadros y las flores, pero sin perder la sobriedad.*

*Lo **specchio** dell'alta cultura balinese. Il disegno dell'hotel e le sue decorazioni sono ricchi d'immagini e fiori ed è ciononostante concentrato.*

Sometimes, only a few steps are needed to end up right in one's own pool. An enticing pleasure for children also. In the spa, exotic aromas and applications put body and soul back in tune.

Manchmal reichen nur wenige Schritte, um direkt im eigenen Pool zu landen. Auch für Kinder ein verlockendes Vergnügen. Im Spa bringen exotische Aromen und Anwendungen Körper und Seele wieder in Einklang.

Quelques pas suffisent parfois pour accéder à la piscine. Pour les enfants aussi, c'est un plaisir alléchant. Dans l'espace spa, les arômes et les traitements exotiques réconcilient le corps et l'esprit.

A veces, tan solo unos pocos pasos son suficientes para pasar directamente a la piscina propia. También para los niños es una diversión tentadora. En el Spa, las aplicaciones y los aromas exóticos contribuyen a la armonía entre el cuerpo y el alma.

A volte bastano pochi passi per arrivare alla propria piscina. Un allettante divertimento anche per i bambini. Nello spa gli aromi esotici e le applicazioni riportano animo e corpo in equilibrio.

Aleenta

Pranburi, Thailand

The possibility to look out over one's own limited horizon continually lures people. This tropical-sweetness is also evoked in Aleenta. A straightforward spot off Thailand's beaten path and yet not far from Bangkok. From the comfortable terrace couches, the ocean seems to be near enough to grasp. All paths to being pampered are short in this family facility—whether to the spa, the restaurant or to one's own tasteful pad. Even paradise seems a bit closer than usual here.

Es ist die Möglichkeit, über den eigenen begrenzten Horizont hinauszublicken, die die Menschen immer wieder lockt. Auch in Aleenta klingt diese tropisch-süße Verheißung an. Ein überschaubarer Platz, abseits der ausgetretenen Pfade Thailands und doch unweit von Bangkok. Von der Terrassenliege aus wirkt das Meer zum Greifen nahe. Alle Wege zum Verwöhnen sind in dieser familiären Anlage kurz – ob zum Spa, zum Restaurant oder zur eigenen, stilvollen Bleibe. Da erscheint selbst das Paradies ein kleines Stück näher als sonst.

Avoir la possibilité d'élargir ses horizons, voilà ce qui attire beaucoup de gens. A Aleente, cette promesse a des sonorités douces et tropicales. Une propriété de taille appréciable, située à l'écart des chemins battus de Thaïland et cependant à proximité de Bangkok. Depuis les chaises longues de la terrasse, la mer semble être à portée de main. Dans cette propriété décontractée, tous les chemins menant aux différents plaisirs sont courts – que vous souhaitiez rejoindre l'espace spa, le restaurant ou votre logement plein de style. Là-bas, même le paradis semble plus accessible qu'ailleurs.

Precisamente la posibilidad de traspasar el propio y limitado horizonte es lo que seduce a las personas una y otra vez. También Aleenta evoca esta dulce promesa tropical. Un lugar manejable, alejado de las sendas más recorridas de Tailandia y aun así, a poca distancia de Bangkok. Acostados en las cómodas tumbonas de la terraza, el mar parece tan cerca y palpable. Todos los caminos que conducen al exquisito trato en este resort de ambiente familiar, son cortos —ya sea para llegar al Spa, al restaurante o al propio elegante alojamiento. Aquí el paraíso parece estar un poco más cerca de lo habitual.

È l'opportunità di guardare oltre al proprio limitato orizzonte che attira la gente. Pure ad Aleenta si sente questa promessa tropicale e dolce. Un posto di facile orientamento, lontano dalle strade battute della Tailandia ed allo stesso tempo vicino a Bangkok. Dal comodo lettino sulla terrazza, il mare sembra vicino da toccare. Tutte le strade per farsi viziare sono corte in quest'impianto di gestione familiare – sia per andare nello spa, sia al ristorante o al proprio alloggio ricco di stile. Così addirittura il paradiso sembra essere un pò più vicino di quanto è normalmente.

Each pavilion is an independent creation and opens marvelous views of the wide Indian Ocean.

Jeder Pavillon ist eine eigenständige Kreation und eröffnet herrliche Aussichten auf den weiten indischen Ozean.

Chaque pavillon est une création particulière et offre une vue imprenable sur l'infini de l'océan Indien.

Cada pabellón es una creación independiente y ofrece una hermosa vista del inmenso Océano Índico.

Ogni padiglione è una creazione di per sé ed apre vedute meravigliose sul vasto Oceano Indiano.

The typical thatched roofs call attention to themselves from inside also. Whether on paths, pool or restaurant—cultivated, family styles determine life in Aleenta.

Die typischen strohgedeckten Dächer ziehen auch im Inneren den Blick auf sich. Ob auf den Wegen, am Pool oder im Restaurant — gepflegter, familiärer Stil bestimmen das Leben in Aleenta.

Même depuis l'intérieur, les toits de paille, typiques de cette région, attirent l'attention. Que vous soyez sur les chemins, dans la piscine ou au restaurant – un style soigné et décontracté caractérise la vie à Aleenta.

Los típicos techos cubiertos de paja atraen la atención también al interior del resort. Trátese de los senderos, la piscina o el restaurante, el estilo elegante y familiar determina el ambiente en Aleenta.

I tetti tipicamente ricoperti di paglia attraggono lo sguardo anche dall'interno. Sia lungo i sentieri, sia nella piscina o nel ristorante – lo stile curato famigliare determina la vita ad Aleenta.

Ana Mandara Resort

Nha Trang, Vietnam

Rampant dark green jungle, evergreen mountain forests, waterfalls and manifold forked watercourse—the South Vietnamese landscape is reflected in the architecture and coloration of the Ana Mandara. With its low buildings made from local precious wood seeming to duck into the luxuriant vegetation the 68-room resort resembles a traditional Vietnamese village. One enjoys a wide view of the Bay of Nha Trang on the South China Sea from all rooms.

Dunkelgrün wuchernder Dschungel, immergrüne Bergwälder, Wasserfälle und vielfältig verzweigte Wasserläufe – das Landschaftsbild Südvietnams spiegelt sich in der Architektur und Farbgestaltung des Ana Mandara wider. Mit seinen niedrigen Häusern aus heimischen Edelhölzern, die sich in die üppige Vegetation zu ducken scheinen, gleicht das 68-Zimmer-Resort einem traditionellen vietnamesischen Dorf. Von fast allen Zimmern aus genießt man einen weiten Blick über die Bucht von Nha Trang auf das südchinesische Meer.

Une jungle foisonnante vert-foncé, des forêts de montagne toujours vertes et un dense réseau de cours d'eau – les paysages du Sud du Vietnam se retrouvent dans l'architecture et les teintes de l'Ana Mandara. Avec ses maisons basses en bois précieux, originaire de la région, qui semblent se cacher au milieu de la végétation envahissante, ce domaine riche de 68 chambres ressemble à un village vietnamien traditionnel. Depuis presque toutes les chambres, on a une vue dégagée de la baie de Nha Trang à la mer de Chine méridionale.

Exuberantes selvas de color verde oscuro, bosques perennes, cascadas y variadas corrientes de agua ramificadas –el paisaje del sur de Vietnam se refleja en la arquitectura y los colores del Ana Mandara. Con sus chalés bajos, construidos con maderas preciosas del lugar, que parecen empequeñecerse en la exuberante vegetación, este resort de 68 habitaciones se asemeja a un tradicional pueblo vietnamita. Desde casi todas las habitaciones se puede disfrutar de una amplia vista del Mar del Sur de China, sobre la bahía de Nha Trang.

Una giungla che cresce rigogliosamente in un verde scuro, boschi di montagna sempre verdi, cascate e corsi d'acqua ramificati – i paesaggi del Vietnam meridionale si trovano riflessi nell'architettura e le colorazioni usate nell'Ana Mandara. Con le sue basse case fatte di legni pregiati locali, che sembrano volersi nascondere nella rigogliosa vegetazione, il resort con 68 camere assomiglia ad un villaggio tipico vietnamese. Quasi tutte le camere danno un ampio panorama sulla baia di Nha Trang ed il mare Sud-cinese.

As the lone hotel, the resort lies directly on the sandy beach of the picturesque former colonial city of Nha Trang.

Als einziges Hotel liegt das Resort direkt am Sandstrand der malerischen ehemaligen Kolonialstadt Nha Trang.

Ce domaine est l'unique hôtel a être situé directement à proximité de la plage de la pittoresque ville autrefois coloniale de Nha Trang.

Como único hotel, el resort se encuentra directamente en la playa de arena de la pintoresca y antigua ciudad colonial de Nha Trang.

Come unico hotel, il resort si trova direttamente sulla spiaggia di sabbia della pittoresca città coloniale di una volta di Nha Trang.

150　　Ana Mandara Resort　*Nha Trang, Vietnam*

The authentic furnishings including handmade furniture and accessories were awarded prizes.

Die authentische Einrichtung mit in Handarbeit gefertigten Möbeln und Accessoires wurde preisgekrönt.

L'aménagement authentique, constitué de meubles et d'accessoires faits à la main a été primé.

El auténtica decoración con muebles y accesorios artesanales ha sido premiada.

L'arredamento autentico con mobili ed accessori fatti a mano è stato premiato.

Bedarra Island

North Queensland, Australia

Only 16 villas belong to the resort and are—fit into the woods as pavilions—spread over a spacious estate. Large wood and glass surfaces characterize the appearance; the modern bungalow architecture, allowing open-style living, is designed to allow the greatest possible views. Surfboards, catamarans, and gourmet picnic baskets are available for leisure-time activities.

Zu dem Resort gehören nur 16 Villen, die sich – als Pavillons in den Wald eingefügt – über ein weitläufiges Gelände verteilen. Große Holz- und Glasflächen bestimmen ihr Erscheinungsbild; die moderne Bungalow-Architektur, die ein offenes Wohnen ermöglicht, stellt sich ganz in den Dienst einer maximalen Aussicht. Für die Freizeitgestaltung stehen Surfbretter, Katamarane und Gourmet-Picknickkörbe zur Verfügung.

Seules 16 villas appartiennent au domaine. Celles-ci – des pavillons intégrés à la forêt – sont dispersées sur un vaste terrain. Leur apparence est caractérisée par de grandes surfaces en bois et en verre ; L'architecture moderne des bungalows, conçue pour vivre dans des espaces ouverts, a pour but d'assurer une vue maximale vers l'extérieur. Des surfs, des catamarans et des paniers de piques-niques pour gourmets sont mis à disposition pour les loisirs.

Este resort dispone tan sólo de 16 chalés, distribuidos en pabellones inmersos en el bosquer –a lo largo y ancho de un vasto recinto. Grandes superficies de madera y cristal definen su apariencia. La moderna arquitectura de los bungalows con su estilo abierto, ofrece una vista panorámica sin límites. Para entretenerse durante el tiempo libre están disponibles tablas de surf, catamaranes y cestos de picnic para sibaritas.

Fanno parte del resort solo 16 ville che sono distribuite su un vasto terreno ed inserite nel bosco, sotto forma di padiglioni. Grandi superfici di legno e di vetro determinano la loro presenza, la moderna architettura dei bungalow che rende possibile l'abitare in un ambiente aperto si mettono al servizio del massimo panorama possibile. Per passare il tempo libero sono a disposizione tavole da surf, catamaran e cesti per picnic da buongustaio.

The interior rooms are presented in modern, unpretentious elegance.

Die Innenräume präsentieren sich in moderner, unprätentiöser Eleganz.

Les espaces intérieurs se présentent dans une élégance moderne et distinguée.

Las áreas comunes al interior del resort dan fe de una elegancia moderna y sin pretensiones.

I locali interni si presentano con un'eleganza moderna e non pretenziosa.

Trees filter the view of the sea, which the guests can enjoy from the pavilions.

Bäume filtern die Aussicht auf das Meer, die der Gast von den Pavillons aus genießen kann.

Des arbres filtrent la vue sur la mer que l'hôte peut apprécier depuis les pavillons.

Los árboles filtran la vista al mar de la que el huésped puede disfrutar desde los pabellones.

Gli alberi filtrano la vista sul mare che l'ospite può godere guardando fuori dei padiglioni.

Bedarra Island *North Queensland, Australia*   155

Vatulele Island Resort

Vatulele Island, Fiji Islands

The resort lies on one of the southern Fiji islands and enables escape from daily life in complete seclusion: neither telephone, newspaper, radio nor television tear the guest out of the holiday mood and only 900 people live on the entire island. The individual resort buildings resemble simple huts and stand between trees on the beach, protected from overly powerful waves by a lagoon. The peak of privacy is the chance to have a "Dinner for Two" on a small island in the lagoon.

Das Resort liegt auf einer der südlichen Fiji-Inseln und bietet die Chance, in völliger Abgeschiedenheit dem Alltag zu entfliehen: Weder Telefon noch Zeitung, Radio oder Fernsehen reißen den Gast aus der Urlaubsstimmung, und auf der ganzen Insel leben nur 900 Menschen. Die einzelnen Gebäude des Resorts erinnern an einfache Hütten und stehen zwischen Bäumen am Strand, der durch eine Lagune vor zu starkem Seegang geschützt ist. Gipfel der Privatheit ist die Möglichkeit eines „Dinner for Two" auf einer kleinen Insel in der Lagune.

Le domaine est situé sur une des îles méridionales des Fiji et a la chance d'offrir la possibilité de s'isoler complètement du quotidien : ni le téléphone, ni journaux, radio ou télévision ne sont susceptibles de troubler l'hôte durant ses congés ; 900 personnes seulement résident sur l'île. Les différents bâtiments du domaine rappellent de simples cabanes et se trouvent entre les arbres, au bord d'une plage, protégée des caprices de la houle par une lagune. Le sommet de l'intimité est la possibilité de goûter au plaisir d'un « dîner à deux » sur une petite île de la lagune.

El resort está ubicado en una de las islas del sur de Fiji y ofrece la posibilidad de escapar de la cotidianidad en un retiro absoluto: Ni el teléfono ni los diarios, ni la radio o la televisión logran arrebatarle al huésped su espíritu vacacional. En toda la isla viven tan sólo 900 personas. Cada una de las edificaciones del resort nos evocan cabañas sencillas. Están situadas entre árboles en la playa, que se encuentra protegida de las fuertes marejadas por una laguna. La privacidad máxima se logra disfrutando de un "dinner for two" en un islote dentro de la laguna.

Il resort si trova su una delle isole Fiji meridionali ed offre l'opportunità di scappare alla vita quotidiana in assoluta solitudine. Non esiste né telefono, né giornale, né radio o tv che possano strappare l'ospite dall'atmosfera di vacanza. Su tutta l'isola vivono soltanto 900 persone. I singoli edifici del resort ricordano semplici capanne e si trovano tra gli alberi sulla spiaggia protetta da una risacca troppo forte grazie ad una laguna. Il massimo della privatezza consiste nella possibilità di poter fare un "Dinner for Two" su una piccola isola in mezzo alla laguna.

The high ceilings ensure pleasant temperatures in the rooms when one wants to recuperate from the day's activities, such as diving.

Die hohen Decken sorgen für angenehme Temperaturen in den Räumen, wenn man sich abends von den Tagesaktivitäten, etwa dem Tauchen, erholen möchte.

Le soir, les hauts plafonds assurent une température agréable dans les chambres et permettent de se reposer des activités de la journée, comme la plongée.

Los altos techos brindan agradables temperaturas en las habitaciones y áreas comunes, cuando se desea descansar por las tardes después de las actividades del día, como por ejemplo, el submarinismo.

Gli alti soffitti fanno mantenere temperature gradevoli nei locali quando ci si vuole riposare la sera dalle attività quotidiane come ad esempio l'immersione.

The guesthouses duck inconspicuously between the shade-giving palm trees on the beach.

Die Gästehäuser ducken sich unauffällig zwischen die Schatten spendenden Palmen am Strand.

Les maisons d'hôte se tapissent, bien cachées, entre les ombres dispensées par les palmiers de la plage.

Las cabañas se esconden discretamente entre las palmas que ofrecen sombra en la playa.

I padiglioni degli ospiti si nascondono sotto palme ombreggianti sulla spiaggia.

Bora Bora Nui Resort & Spa

Bora Bora, French Polynesia

Visitors to the resort can choose between various accommodations. Part of the 120 villas stand on the luxuriantly overgrown, terraced slopes of a hilly terrain, another in the middle of crystal clear water in a small inlet. Common to all is the view of a lagoon in the South Pacific, a bathroom made of Italian marble, and a four-posted bed made from mahogany. In the water villas, the guest can watch the happenings in the sea through a glass window in the living area.

Wer das Resort besucht, kann zwischen verschiedenen Unterkünften wählen. Ein Teil der 120 Villen steht an den üppig bewachsenen, terrassierten Hängen eines hügeligen Geländes, ein anderer mitten im glasklaren Wasser einer kleinen Bucht. Allen gemeinsam sind die Aussicht auf eine Lagune im Südpazifik, ein Badezimmer aus italienischem Marmor und ein Himmelbett aus Mahagoni. In den Wasservillen kann der Gast durch ein Glasfenster im Boden des Wohnbereichs das Treiben im Meer beobachten.

Celui qui viendra visiter le domaine pourra choisir entre différents logements. Une partie des 120 villas se trouvent sur les flancs en terrasse foisonnant de végétation de la colline, une autre partie se trouve au milieu d'une petite baie à l'eau claire. Tous ces logements ont en commun une vue imprenable sur la lagune du Pacifique Sud, une salle de bain en marbre italien et un lit en baldaquin en acajou. Dans les villas du bord de l'eau, l'hôte peut observer par une fenêtre posée au sol de l'espace habitable l'activité des habitants de la mer.

El visitante que llega a este resort, puede elegir entre diferentes alojamientos. Una parte de los 120 chalés se encuentra en las exuberantes laderas escalonadas de un terreno con colinas, y, la otra, en medio de las aguas cristalinas de una pequeña bahía. Todas tienen en común la vista hacia una laguna del Pacífico Sur, un baño de mármol italiano y una cama de caoba con dosel. En los chalés de la pequeña bahía, el huésped puede apreciar el movimiento del mar a través de una superficie de cristal en el suelo de la sala de estar.

Chi visita il resort, potrà scegliere tra diversi alloggi. Una parte delle 120 ville si trova in una zona collinare, su pendii dotati di terrazze e con una rigogliosa vegetazione, l'altra parte in mezzo all'acqua limpida di una piccola baia. Tutte hanno in comune la vista su una laguna nel Pacifico meridionale, una stanza da bagno di marmo italiano ed un letto a baldacchino di mogano. Nelle ville sull'acqua, l'ospite può osservare la vita sottomarina da una finestra nel pavimento della zonas oggiorno.

The guests in this resort can feel fine like a fish in water—almost literally.

Wohlfühlen wie ein Fisch im Wasser können sich die Gäste dieses Resorts – fast im wahrsten Sinne des Wortes.

Les clients de ce domaine se sentiront bien comme des poissons dans l'eau – presque au sens propre de l'expression.

Los huéspedes de este resort pueden sentirse como pez en el agua – casi en el más estricto sentido de la expresión.

Gli ospiti di questo resort si possono sentire bene come un pesce nell'acqua – quasi letteralmente.

Much wood lends the guesthouses a certain kind of coziness—inside and out.

Viel Holz verleiht den Gästehäusern ein gewisses Maß an Gemütlichkeit   innen wie außen.

Le bois communique aux maisons d'hôte un certain confort – à l'intérieur comme à l'extérieur.

La abundancia de madera le otorga a las cabañas una cierta dosis de calidez –tanto al interior como al exterior.

L'utilizzo di molto legno dona ai padiglioni degli ospiti una certa comodità – all'interno ed all'esterno.

Beit al Bahar Villas

Dubai, United Arab Emirates

House on the sea is the simple meaning of the Arabian name of the 19 ochre adobe villas situated directly on the white fine-grained sandy Jumeirah beach. With their gardens and private pools protected by walls, they are a genuine sanctuary. Architecture and design are oriented on Dubai's Arabian legacy. In the interior, dark wood, worked with extravagant ornaments, and precious fabrics in warm Burgundy and golden hues dominate.

Haus am Meer – nichts anderes bedeutet der arabische Name der 19 ockerfarbenen, aus Lehmziegeln gebauten Villen, die direkt am feinkörnigen weißen Sandstrand von Jumeirah Beach liegen. Mit ihren durch Mauern geschützten Gärten und Privatpools sind sie ein wahres Refugium. Architektur und Design orientieren sich am arabischen Erbe Dubais. Im Inneren dominieren dunkles, mit aufwendigen Ornamenten bearbeitetes Holz und kostbare Stoffe in warmen Burgund- und Goldtönen.

Une maison du bord de mer – voilà ce que signifie en arabe le nom des 19 villas de couleur ocre construites en briques d'argile situées directement au bord de la plage de sable extra fin de Jumeirah Beach. Avec leurs jardins et piscines privées entourés de murs, elles offre un vrai refuge. L'architecture et le design s'inspirent de l'héritage arabe de Dubay. Dans les espaces intérieurs, dominent un bois sombre, décoré avec des ornements chargés, et des étoffes de grande valeur dans les tons chauds d'or et de bordeaux.

"Casa en la playa" significa el nombre en árabe de los 19 chalés de color ocre, construidos en adobe y ubicados directamente en la playa de arena fina de Jumeirah. Con sus jardines y piscinas protegidos por muros, estos chalés son un verdadero refugio. La arquitectura y el diseño recogen el patrimonio árabe de Dubai. En los espacios interiores predominan la madera oscura, tallada con complejos ornamentos, y valiosas telas en cálidos tonos burdeos y dorados.

Casa sul mare – è questo il significato del nome arabo delle 19 ville costruite di tegole d'argilla e di colore ocra che si trovano direttamente sulla spiaggia a sabbia fine e bianca di Jumeirah Beach. Con i suoi giardini e le piscine private protette da muri rappresentano un vero rifugio. L'architettura ed il design si orientano sull'eredità araba di Dubai. All'interno dominano il legno scuro lavorato rigogliosamente e stoffe pregiate dalle tonalità calde in rosso scuro e d'oro.

Tempting contrast: the traditionally constructed villas against the background of the spectacular silhouette of the Burj Al Arab sister hotel.

Reizvoller Kontrast: Die traditionell gebauten Villen vor der spektakulären Silhouette des Schwesterhotels Burj Al Arab.

Contraste impressionnant : les villas à l'architecture traditionnelle à proximité de la silhouette spectaculaire des deux tours jumelles de l'hôtel Burj Al Arab.

Un contraste encantador: Los chalés de construcción tradicional delante de la espectacular silueta del hotel hermano, Burj Al Arab.

Un contrasto grazioso: le ville costruite in modo tradizionale davanti alla spettacolare silhouette dell'hotel sorella Burj Al Arab.

The color scheme and much dark wood emphasize the oriental opulent ambience in the spacious rooms.

Die Farbgebung und viel dunkles Holz unterstreichen das orientalisch üppige Ambiente in den groß-zügigen Räumen.

Les tons et l'utilisation de beaucoup de bois sombre souligne l'exubérante ambiance orientale des généreux espaces.

El colorido y la abundancia de madera oscura acentúan el exuberante ambiente oriental en los amplios salones.

Le colorazioni e molto legno scuro sottolineano l'ambiente opulento nelle stanze di dimensioni generose.

One&Only Royal Mirage

Dubai, United Arab Emirates

Strictly speaking, the facility consists of three different hotels: the Palace with 226 rooms, the 32-room Residence & Spa, conceived as an exclusive club, and the 162-room Arabian Court, completed in 2003. Together, they result in a genuine small holiday village with eleven restaurants and bars, inviting one to go out and explore. One of the highlights is the wellness center with the Hammam and Givenchy Spa. The facility architecture lets one perceive the joy of Arabian décor.

Genau genommen besteht die Anlage aus drei verschiedenen Hotels: dem Palace mit 226 Zimmern, dem als exklusiven Club konzipierten Residence & Spa mit 32 Zimmern und dem 2003 fertig gestellten Arabian Court mit 162 Zimmern. Zusammen ergeben sie ein richtiges kleines Feriendorf mit elf Restaurants und Bars, das zu Entdeckungsreisen einlädt. Eines der Highlights ist das Wellnesszentrum mit Hammam und Givenchy Spa. Die Architektur der Anlage lässt die Freude an arabischem Dekor erkennen.

Le domaine est constitué de trois hôtels différents : le Palace qui contient 226 chambres, le domaine Résidence & Spa, conçu comme un club exclusif contenant 32 chambres et le Arabian Court contenant 162 chambres dont la réalisation sera terminé en 2003. Ensemble, ils constituent un vrai petit village de vacances avec onze restaurants et bars, qui invitent à des voyages de découverte. Une des attractions est le centre de bien-être doté d'un hammam et un spa Givenchy. L'architecte de l'ensemble laisse transparaître une certaine attirance pour les décors arabes.

Para ser exactos, este resort está compuesto por tres hoteles diferentes: El Palace, con 226 habitaciones, el Residence & Spa, concebido como un exclusivo club, con 32 habitaciones, y el Arabian Court, con 162 habitaciones, terminado de construir en el 2003. En conjunto, forman un verdadero pequeño complejo turístico, con once restaurantes y bares, que invita al huésped a un viaje de exploración. Una de las principales atracciones es el centro de wellness con baño turco y Givenchy Spa. La arquitectura del resort demuestra el interés y gusto por la decoración árabe.

Per esattezza l'impianto consiste in tre hotel diversi: il Palace con 226 camere, il Residence & Spa concepito come club esclusivo con 32 camere e l'Arabian Court che è stato costruito nel 2003 con 162 camere. Insieme formano un vero piccolo villaggio di vacanze con undici ristoranti e bar che invitano ad essere scoperti. Uno dei clou è il centro wellness con Hammam e Givenchy Spa. L'architettura dell'impianto fa intuire la gioia di utilizzare decorazioni arabe.

Especially the windows, with their pointed arches or ornamental tracery, ensure an oriental atmosphere.

Vor allem die Fenster sorgen mit Spitzbogen oder ornamentalem Maßwerk für eine orientalische Atmosphäre.

L'atmosphère orientale est surtout rendue par les fenêtres et leurs arcs en ogive ou les grilles ornementales.

En especial las ventanas, con sus arcos ojivales y tracería ornamental, proporcionan un ambiente oriental.

Soprattutto le finestre provvedono a creare l'atmosfera orientale con archi ottusi e lavorazioni ornamentali.

The Rooftop Lounge in the Arabian Court is one of the favorite in-meeting-spots in Jumeirah Beach at sunset.

Die Rooftop Lounge des Arabian Court ist in Jumeirah Beach einer der beliebtesten Szenetreffs zum Sonnenuntergang.

A l'heure du crépuscule, le Rooftop Lounge du Arabian Court est un des lieux de rencontre les plus apprécié à Jumeirah Beach.

El Rooftoop Lounge del Hotel Arabian Court es en Jumeirah Beach uno de los lugares de encuentro predilectos de la jet set del lugar para apreciar la puesta del sol.

La Rooftop Lounge dell'Arabian Court è uno dei locali di scena più amati per l'ora del tramonto.

One&Only Royal Mirage *Dubai, United Arab Emirates*   171

Four Seasons Resort Sharm El Sheikh

Sharm El Sheikh, Egypt

The interplay between desert and sea constitutes the special atmosphere of this luxury resort on the southern tip of the Sinai Peninsula. 1800 palm trees were planted to turn the small coastal strip in front of the jagged rock formations of the Sinai Mountains into an oasis. The guest villas with their 136 rooms and suites are grouped around an idyllic inner courtyard with murmuring fountains. Moorish arched windows, rich ornaments and mosaics emphasize the Oriental ambience.

Das Zusammenspiel von Wüste und Meer macht die besondere Atmosphäre dieses Luxusresorts an der Südspitze der Sinaihalbinsel aus. 1800 Palmen wurden angepflanzt, um aus dem schmalen Küstenstreifen vor den schroffen Felsformationen des Sinaigebirges eine Oase entstehen zu lassen. Die Gästevillen mit den 136 Zimmern und Suiten gruppieren sich um idyllische Innenhöfe mit plätschernden Brunnen. Maurische Bogenfenster, reiche Ornamente und Mosaike unterstreichen das orientalische Ambiente.

La coexistence du désert et de la mer créent l'atmosphère toute particulière de ce domaine luxurieux situé à la pointe Sud de la presqu'île du Sinaï. 1800 palmiers furent plantés afin de transformer en oasis la mince plage située devant les rudes rochers de la montagne du Sinaï. Les villas des hôtes, dotées de 136 chambres et suites se groupent autour de cours intérieurs idylliques, dotées de fontaines rafraîchissantes. Des arc de fenêtres mauresques, de riches ornements et des mosaïques soulignent l'ambiance orientale.

La combinación de desierto y mar es lo que proporciona el especial ambiente a este resort de lujo en el extremo sur de la península del Sinaí. 1800 palmas fueron plantadas para convertir en un oasis la estrecha faja costera, delante de las escarpadas formaciones rocosas de las montañas del Sinaí. Las edificaciones, con un total de 136 habitaciones y suites, se agrupan alrededor de idílicos patios interiores con fuentes murmurantes. Ventanas en forma de arco de estilo morisco, lujosos ornamentos y mosaicos acentúan la atmósfera oriental.

L'interazione tra il deserto ed il mare fa la particolare atmosfera di questo resort di lusso sulla punta meridionale della peninsola del Sinai. 1800 palme sono state piantate per far diventare un'oasi la stretta costa che si trova davanti alle aspre formazioni rocciose delle montagne del Sinai. Le ville degli ospiti con 136 camere e suites si raggruppano attorno a cortili interni idillici con gorgoglianti fontane, finestre maure ad archi ottusi, ricchi ornamenti e mosaici che sottolineano l'ambiente orientale.

Dining with a view of the diver's paradise—the Red Sea.

Dinieren mit Blick auf das Taucherparadies Rotes Meer.

Dînez ici et admirez la vue sur le paradis des plongeurs de la mer Rouge.

Una cena con vista al paraiso del submarinismo, el Mar Rojo.

Cenare con la vista sul paradiso dell'immersione del Mar Rosso.

Through its restrained color scheme, the interior seems to have oriental elegance, without being florid.

Durch die zurückhaltende Farbgebung wirkt das Interieur orientalisch elegant, ohne überladen zu sein.

Grâce à la retenue des teintes, l'intérieur oriental apparaît élégant sans être chargé.

Gracias al sobrio colorido de los espacios interiores se logra un efecto oriental elegante y no recargado.

Grazie al discreto utilizzo dei colori, gli arredamenti si presentano con l'eleganza orientale senza essere sovraccarichi.

The Chedi Muscat

Muscat, Oman

On the rim of Oman's capitol Muscat lies the Chedi, a complex ensemble of white buildings that can remind the observer of the Alhambra, if it were not for the modern architecture. The courtyard awaits with its intricate system of pools, a water garden lies in front of the restaurant. But the facility is in no way introverted; rather all rooms offer a fascinating view, either of the Indian Ocean or of the nearby mountains. A private beach also belongs to the hotel.

Am Rande von Omans Hauptstadt Muscat liegt das Chedi, ein komplexes Ensemble strahlend weißer Gebäude, das den Betrachter an die Alhambra erinnern könnte, wäre da nicht die moderne Architektur. Die Innenhöfe warten mit einem verschlungenen System von Teichen auf, vor dem Restaurant liegt ein Wassergarten. Doch die Anlage ist keineswegs introvertiert, vielmehr bieten alle Zimmer eine faszinierende Aussicht, entweder auf den Indischen Ozean oder auf die nahegelegenen Berge. Ein Privatstrand gehört ebenfalls zum Hotel.

Dans la périphérie de la capitale de l'Oman, Muscat, est situé le Chedi, un ensemble complexe de bâtiments d'un blanc rayonnant, qui rappelle au visiteur l'Alhambra, sans parler du caractère moderne de l'architecture. Les cours intérieurs offrent un système complexe et sinueux de bassins ; devant le restaurant se trouve un jardin d'eau. Cependant, le domaine n'est pas du tout replié sur lui-même ; toutes les fenêtres offrent une vue fascinante soit sur l'océan Indien, soit sur les montagnes voisines. L'hôtel possède aussi une plage privée.

Al borde de la capital de Omán, Muscat, está ubicado The Chedi, un conjunto de construcciones de radiante blancura que podría traer a la memoria del observador el palacio de la Alhambra, si no fuera por la arquitectura moderna. Los patios interiores presentan un complejo sistema de estanques y delante del restaurante se encuentra un jardín acuático. No obstante, el resort no está en absoluto encerrado en sí mismo; todas las habitaciones ofrecen una vista fascinante del Océano Índico o de las montañas cercanas. El hotel también cuenta con una playa privada.

Ai bordi della capitale dell'Oman Muscat si trova Chedi, un insieme complesso d'edifici bianchi splendenti che all'ospite potrebbe ricordare l'Alhambra, se non fosse per l'architettura moderna. I cortili interni si presentano con un sistema intrecciato di stagni, davanti al ristorante si trova un giardino d'acqua. L'impianto tuttavia non è introverso, poiché tutte le camere offrono un panorama affascinante sull'Oceano Indiano oppure sulle vicine montagne. Una spiaggia privata fa altresì parte dell'hotel.

The "De-Luxe Rooms" are designed to be exceptionally unpretentious and tasteful, almost puristic.

Außergewöhnlich schlicht und geschmackvoll, beinahe puristisch sind die De-Luxe Rooms gestaltet.

Les chambres de-Luxe sont aménagées de façon extrêmement sobre et du meilleur goût, presque puriste.

Las habitaciones De-Luxe están diseñadas con gusto y de manera extremadamente sencilla, casi purista.

Le camere De-Luxe sono state create in modo straordinariamente semplice e di gusto, quasi in modo puristico.

The bathrooms in the suites are not characterized by oriental splendor, but by apparently Asian asceticism.

Die Baderäume in den Suiten zeichnen sich nicht durch orientalischen Prunk aus, sondern durch asiatisch anmutende Askese.

Les espaces de bain des suites ne se démarquent pas par le faste oriental mais par une ascèse asiatique modeste.

Los baños de la suites no se distinguen por una fastuosidad oriental, sino más bien por un elegante ascetismo asiático.

Le stanze da bagno non si distinguono per un fasto orientale, ma per un'askesi che sembra asiatica.

The cuddly scenery in the lobby lounge ensures an Arabian flair.

Für arabisches Flair sorgt auch die Kuschellandschaft in der Lobby-Lounge.

Un tapis de coussin contribue à l'atmosphère arabe au lobby-lounge.

El ambiente árabe lo proporciona también el paisaje acogedor de cojines y almohadones en el lounge del vestíbulo.

Pure l'arredamento coccolante nella Lobby Lounge fa sentire il fascino arabo.

Le Prince Maurice

Poste de Flacq, Mauritius

The property lies on a peninsula on the northeast coast of Mauritius, in the midst of luxuriant exotic vegetation. It attempts to evoke times past when seaman still landed here to trade spices: modern elements such as a computer at the reception desk were skillfully concealed behind sheets of glass and the room keys kept in two wooden chests. Differing suites can be chosen, the largest measures 350 m² and offers a private patio, an open-air bath and two pools.

Auf einer Halbinsel an der Nordostküste von Mauritius liegt das Anwesen inmitten üppiger exotischer Vegetation. Es versucht vergangene Zeiten heraufzubeschwören, als noch Seefahrer wegen des Gewürzhandels hier anlegten: Moderne Elemente wie der Computer an der Rezeption werden geschickt hinter dunklen Glasplatten verborgen und die Zimmerschlüssel in zwei Holztruhen aufbewahrt. Unterschiedliche Suiten stehen zur Auswahl, die größte misst 350 m² und bietet einen privaten Patio, ein Open-Air-Bad und zwei Pools.

Le domaine se trouve sur une presqu'île, sur la côte Nord-est de l'île Maurice, et est situé au milieu d'une végétation exotique dense. Il évoque les temps anciens alors que les marins débarquaient ici pour faire le commerce des épices : les éléments modernes comme l'ordinateur de la réception sont cachés derrière des plaques de verre assombries et les clés des chambres conservées dans deux males en bois. Différentes suites peuvent être choisies ; la plus grande a une taille de 350 m² et est dotée d'un patio privé, d'une salle de bain en plein air et de deux piscines.

En una península, en la costa noreste de Mauricio, está ubicado este hotel, en medio de una exuberante vegetación exótica. El establecimiento intenta evocar épocas pasadas, cuando los marineros anclaban aquí, debido al comercio de especias. Elementos de la modernidad, como el ordenador en la recepción, se esconden hábilmente tras placas de vidrio oscuro y las llaves de las habitaciones se mantienen en un cofre de madera. Hay diferentes suites para elegir y la más grande de éstas es de 350 m² y cuenta con un patio interior privado, bañera a cielo raso y dos piscinas.

La tenuta si trova su una peninsola sulla costa Nord-Est di Mauritius, in mezzo ad una rigogliosa vegetazione esotica. Si tenta d'evocare i tempi passati quando i marinai vi approdavano per il commercio delle spezie. Elementi moderni come i computer della reception sono stati nascosti dietro a piastre di vetro scuro e le chiavi delle camere sono depositate in due cassoni di legno. Sono a disposizione diverse suites, la più grande misura 350 m² e offre un patio privato, un bagno all'aperto e due piscine.

Rough-hewn stones on the wall and wood and straw on the roofs create an authentic natural atmosphere.

Grob behauener Stein an der Wand sowie Holz und Stroh auf dem Dach schaffen eine authentisch-natürliche Atmosphäre.

Les pierres grossièrement taillées des murs ainsi que le bois et la paille sur le toit créent une atmosphère authentique et naturelle.

La piedra labrada toscamente en las paredes, así como la madera y la paja en los techos, logran crear un auténtico ambiente natural.

Pietre grezzamente lavorate sui muri, nonché legno e paglia sul tetto creano un'atmosfera autentica e naturale.

Not only a pool, sauna, steam bath and plunge-pool are available for enhancing fitness and well-being, but even an air-conditioned squash court.

Um Fitness und Wohlbefinden zu steigern, stehen nicht nur Pool, Sauna, Dampfbad und Tauchbecken bereit, sondern auch ein klimatisierter Squash-Court.

Afin d'augmenter l'offre en fitness et en bien-être, on trouve à sa disposition non seulement une piscine, un sauna et un bain de vapeur et un bassin de plongée, mais aussi un court de squash climatisé.

Para mejorar el estado físico y sentirse bien, no sólo están a disposición piscinas, sauna, baños turcos y una pila para sumergirse, sino también un cancha de squash climatizada.

Per aumentare la fitness ed il benessere sono a disposizione non solo piscina, sauna, bagno a vapore e vasca d'immersione, ma anche un squash court climatizzato.

The Residence

Belle Mare, Mauritius

The Residence's architecture reminds one of the colonial age when Mauritius was part of the British Empire. The foyer with its massive pillars revives the splendid glamour of bygone days. Even today, most hotel guests come from Great Britain. Situated on a kilometer long private beach, the buildings are concealed between the trees, fulfilling the tourist office's strict stipulations, demanding that the buildings, regarding size and style, adapt harmoniously to the environs.

Die Architektur des Residence erinnert an die Kolonialzeit, als Mauritius zum britischen Empire gehörte. Die Eingangshalle mit ihren mächtigen Säulen lässt den prunkvollen Glanz jener Tage wieder aufleben. Heute noch sind es vor allem Gäste aus Großbritannien, die das Hotel besuchen. An einem Privatstrand von einem Kilometer Länge gelegen, verbergen sich die Gebäude zwischen den Bäumen. Sie erfüllen die strengen Auflagen des Fremdenverkehrsamts, nach denen Häuser sich in Größe und Bauart in ihre Umbebung harmonisch einfügen müssen.

L'architecture de Residence rappelle l'époque coloniale, alors que l'île Maurice appartenait à l'empire Britannique. Le hall d'entrée avec ses puissantes colonnes fait revivre le faste somptueux de cette époque. Aujourd'hui encore, la majorité des clients de l'hôtel sont originaires de Grande-Bretagne. Situé au bord d'une plage privée d'un kilomètre de longueur, les bâtiments sont cachés entre les arbres. Ils honorent les réglementations pourtant strictes de l'office du tourisme, selon lesquelles les maisons doivent se fondre harmonieusement à leur environnement pour ce qui est leur taille et leur architecture.

La arquitectura del Residence recuerda la época colonial, cuando Mauricio formaba parte del imperio británico. El vestíbulo de entrada, con sus imponentes columnas, hace revivir el pomposo lujo de aquellos tiempos. Aun hoy en día se alojan principalmente visitantes británicos en el hotel. En la playa privada de un kilómetro de largo se ocultan las edificaciones entre los árboles. Éstas cumplen las estrictas normas establecidas por la Oficina de Turismo, según las cuales las construcciones, tanto en tamaño como en tipo de construcción, deben integrarse al entorno de manera armoniosa.

L'architettura del Residence ricorda i tempi coloniali quando Mauritius faceva parte dell'Impero Britannico. L'entrata con le sue maiestose colonne lascia rivivere lo sfarzoso splendore di quei tempi. Oggi sono soprattutto ospiti inglesi a visitare l'hotel. Gli edifici si nascondono tra gli alberi lungo una spiaggia privata di un chilometro di lunghezza. Soddisfano le rigide condizioni dell'ente del turismo, secondo le quali la dimensione e la costruzione delle case si deve integrare armoniosamente ai dintorni.

Having walked through the entrance hall, one gazes across the pool to the ocean.

Wer die Eingangshalle durchschritten hat, blickt über den Pool hinweg aufs Meer.

Après avoir traversé le hall d'entrée, on peut admirer la mer située au-delà de la piscine.

Atravesando el vestíbulo de la entrada se puede apreciar el mar por encima de la piscina.

Chi ha attraversato la lobby vede il mare dietro alla piscina.

Architecture and furnishings abduct the guest into the past times of colonial rule.

Architektur und Ausstattung entführen den Gast in vergangene Zeiten der Kolonialherrschaft.

L'architecture et l'aménagement replongent l'hôte dans les temps passés de la domination coloniale.

La arquitectura y la decoración transportan al huésped a la antigua época del dominio colonial.

L'architettura e l'arredamento portano via l'ospite nei tempi passati dell'impero coloniale.

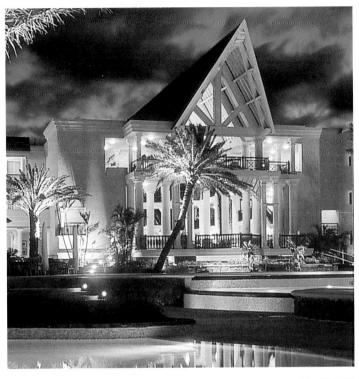

One&Only Le Touessrok

Trou d'Eau Douce, Mauritius

During an extensive renovation that brought modern facilities with furniture by Philippe Starck to the resort, it was also expanded by 98 suites. It is situated on an own small island, connected with the existing buildings via a wooden bridge. Its circular arrangement gives each individual suite a panoramic view of the crystal clear sea. Staggered floors ensure a spacious room impression and the voluminous egg-shaped tubs offer room for a bath as a twosome.

Bei einer umfassenden Renovierung, die dem Resort eine moderne Einrichtung mit Möbeln von Philippe Starck bescherte, wurde es auch gleich um 98 Suiten erweitert. Sie liegen auf einer eigenen kleinen Insel, die über eine Holzbrücke mit den bestehenden Gebäuden verbunden ist. Ihre kreisförmige Anordnung verschafft jeder einzelnen Suite einen Panoramablick auf das kristallklare Meer. Versetzte Geschosse sorgen für einen großzügigen Raumeindruck, und die voluminösen eiförmigen Wannen bieten Platz für ein Bad zu zweit.

A l'occasion d'une importante rénovation, qui a doté le domaine d'un aménagement moderne dont des meubles de Philippe Starck, le domaine a été agrandi et doté de 98 suites supplémentaires. Celles-ci se trouvent sur une petite île à part, reliée au bâtiment déjà existant par un pont de bois. Leur arrangement en forme de cercle permet à chacune des suites de jouir d'une vue panoramique sur une mer cristalline. Des étages en terrasse rendent les espaces plus spacieux, et les baignoires de taille volumineuse permettent de prendre un bain à deux.

En una remodelación total, que le brindó al resort un equipamiento moderno con muebles de Philippe Starck, el hotel fue ampliado con 98 suites. Éstas están situadas en una pequeña isla propia, unidas a la antigua edificación mediante un puente de madera. Su disposición circular le ofrece a cada suite una vista panorámica del mar de aguas cristalinas. Los distintos niveles crean la impresión de un generoso espacio y las inmensas bañeras de forma ovalada ofrecen lugar para dos.

Durante un esteso rinnovamento che ha regalato al resort l'arredamento moderno con mobili di Philippe Starck, l'hotel è stato anche ampliato di 98 suites. Si trovano su una piccola isola che è collegata tramite una passerella di legno con gli edifici esistenti. La disposizione circolare regala ad ognuna delle suites il panorama sul mare cristallino. Piani spostati tra loro provvedono a creare l'impressione di vani di dimensioni generose, le vasche grandi a forma di uovo offrono lo spazio per un bagno in due.

A tiny island lies before the eastern cost of Mauritius, which accommodates part of the resort.

Vor der Ostküste *von Mauritius liegt eine winzige Insel, die einen Teil des Resorts beherbergt.*

Au large *de la côte Est de l'île Maurice se trouve une île minuscule qui accueille une partie du domaine.*

Delante de *la costa oriental de Mauricio se encuentra una diminuta isla que alberga una parte del resort.*

Davanti *alla costa levante di Mauritius si trova una minuscula isola che alloggia una parte del resort.*

The suite furnishings are bright and modern; especially the baths are oriented on modern design trends.

Die Einrichtung der Suiten ist hell und modern, vor allem die Bäder orientieren sich an aktuellen Designtrends.

L'aménagement des suites est claire et moderne ; particulièrement l'aménagement des salles de bains suit les tendances actuelles du design.

La decoración de las suites es moderna y de colores claros, sobre todo los baños acogen las tendencias actuales de diseño.

L'arredamento delle suites è chiaro e moderno e soprattutto le stanze da bagno si orientano sui trend del design contemporaneo.

Banyan Tree Seychelles

Mahé Island, Seychelles

Whether located in the rainforest or on the beach, one sees the Indian Ocean and the fine-grained sandy bay from the white villas—pure postcard cliché. Colonial architecture, ethno-fabrics, and Creole delicacies exude exotic charms. The furniture and accessories were gathered from Africa and Southeast Asia. The legendary Coco de Mer, largest nut in the world, inspired many of the artworks. Even larger are the giant turtles one can meet during a stroll on the beach.

Ob im Regenwald oder direkt am Strand gelegen, von den weißen Villen aus sieht man den Indischen Ozean und die feinsandige Bucht – das reinste Postkartenklischee. Koloniale Architektur, Ethnostoffe und kreolische Delikatessen verbreiten exotischen Charme. Die Möbel und Accessoires sind aus Afrika und Süd-Ost-Asien zusammengetragen. Inspiration für viele Kunstwerke war die legendäre Coco de Mer, die größte Nuss der Welt. Noch größer sind die Riesenschildkröten, denen man beim Strandspaziergang begegnen kann.

Qu'elles soient situées dans la forêt vierge ou directement en bord de mer, toutes les villas blanches donnent sur l'océan Indien et les baies de sable fin – le cliché carte postale typique. L'architecture coloniale, les tissus ethniques et les délicatesses créoles communiquent aux espaces un charme exotique. Les meubles et les accessoires sont originaires d'Afrique ou du Sud-Est asiatique. La coco de mer légendaire, la plus grosse noix du monde, sert d'inspiration à de nombreuses oeuvres d'art. Les tortues géantes que l'on peut voir à l'occasion d'une promenade sur la plage sont encore plus grandes.

Independientemente si se está en la selva lluviosa o en la playa, desde los blancos chalés se divisa el Océano Índico y la bahía de arena fina –el más puro cliché de tarjeta postal. La arquitectura colonial, las telas étnicas y las delicatessen criollas irradian el encanto exótico. Los muebles y los accesorios provienen de África y el sureste asiático. Muchas obras de arte están inspiradas en el legendario coco-de-mer, la nuez más grande del mundo. Más grandes aún son las tortugas gigantes con las que uno se encuentra al salir de paseo.

Che si trovino nella foresta pluviale oppure direttamente sulla spiaggia, dalle bianche ville si vede l'Oceano Indiano e la baia dalla sabbia fine – un vero cliché da cartolina postale. Architettura coloniale, stoffe e prelibatezze creole diffondono lo charme esotico. I mobili e gli accessori provvengono dall'Africa e dal Sud-Est-Asiatico. Ispirazione per molte delle opere d'arte è la leggendaria Coco de Mer, la più grande noce del mondo. Sono ancora più grandi le tartarughe giganti che si possono incontrare durante le passeggiate lungo la spiaggia.

The magnificent pool scenery reaches all the way to the ocean waves in the protected bay.

Die grandiose Poollandschaft reicht bis zur Meeresbrandung in der geschützten Bucht.

Le grandiose paysage de bassin s'étend jusqu'au déferlement des vagues dans la baie protégée.

El grandioso paisaje de piscinas se extiende hasta las olas de la bahía protegida.

Il paesaggio grandioso della piscina arriva fino alla risacca del mare in una baia riparata.

African-inspired *furniture, island art, and straight-lined architecture: the wave washed facility forebodes a stylish vacation.*

Afrikanisch inspiriertes *Mobiliar, Insel-Kunst und gradlinige Architektur: Die von Wellen umspülte Anlage verspricht stilvollen Urlaub.*

Un mobilier *d'inspiration africaine, un art insulaire et une architecture en lignes droites : le domaine, léché par les vagues, vous promet de passer des vacances de grand style.*

Mobiliario de inspiración *africana, arte isleño y una arquitectura sobria: Este resort bañado por las olas promete unas vacaciones con estilo.*

Mobili ispirati *dall'Africa, arte dell'isola ed architettura rettilinea: la tenuta baciata dalle onde promette una vacanza di stile.*

Banyan Tree Seychelles *Mahé Island, Seychelles* 197

Chilli, cloves, and cardamom provide culinary treats in the Saffron Restaurant. The majestic villas guarantee a private sphere.

Chili, Nelken und Kardamom sorgen für kulinarische Genüsse im Restaurant Saffron. Die majestätischen Villen garantieren Privatsphäre.

Au restaurant Saffron, le chili, les clous de girofle et la cardamome vous promettent des plaisirs culinaires. Les majestueuses villas préservent une sphère privée.

Los chiles, los clavos de olor y el cardamomo proporcionan placeres culinarios en el restaurante Saffron. Los majestuosos chalés garantizan privacidad.

Cili, chiodi di garofano e cardamo garantiscono godurie culinarie nel ristorante Saffron. Le ville maiestose invece garantiscono il rispetto della sfera privata.

Frégate Island Private

Frégate Island, Seychelles

Close to the equator, the tiny island lies in the Indian Ocean. Powdery sand on seven beaches surrounds this resort. It has a sensitive ecosystem with rare animal species such as the Frigate bird, famous for its two-meter wingspan and after which the island was named. In the past, it incidentally served as a pirate's hideout and the buccaneers seem to have left their treasures in the villas' living and bedrooms: African hand carved beds, Javanese sculptures, Egyptian cotton.

Nur wenige Grade vom Äquator entfernt liegt die winzige Insel im Indischen Ozean. Puderiger Sand an sieben Stränden umgibt dieses Resort. Es besitzt ein sensibles Ökosystem mit seltenen Tierarten wie dem Frégate-Vogel, der berühmt ist für seine zwei Meter Flügelspannweite und nach dem die Insel benannt ist. Früher diente sie übrigens als Piratenversteck und es scheint so, als hätten die Seeräuber in den Wohn- und Schlafzimmern der Villen ihre Schätze zurückgelassen: Handgeschnitzte Betten aus Afrika, Skulpturen aus Java, Baumwolle aus Ägypten.

Située qu'à quelques degrés de l'équateur, cette île minuscule se trouve dans l'océan Indien. Sept plages au sable fin comme de la poudre entourent ce domaine. Celui-ci possède un écosystème sensible accueillant des espèces animales rares telles que les frégate, oiseau célèbre pour l'envergure de ses ailes, grande de deux mètres, et qui donne son nom à l'île. Celle-ci était utilisée autrefois par les pirates comme cachette ; et il se pourrait bien qu'ils aient laissé leurs trésors dans les chambres et les salons des villas : des lits sculptés à la main originaires d'Afrique, des sculptures de Java, du coton d'Egypte.

A pocos grados de latitud de la línea ecuatorial, se encuentra esta pequeña isla en el Océano Índico. El resort está rodeado de siete playas de fina arena. Posee un ecosistema muy sensible con especies animales raras, como el pájaro fragata, famoso por la envergadura de dos metros de sus alas y del cual la isla adoptó el nombre. Por cierto, ésta sirvió de escondite de piratas y todo parece indicar que éstos hubiesen dejado sus tesoros en las salas y los dormitorios de los chalés: Camas africanas talladas a mano, esculturas de Java, algodón de Egipto.

La minuscola isola si trova a soli pochi gradi dall'Equatore nell'Oceano Indiano. Sabbia fine come la polvere su sette spiagge circonda questo resort. Dispone di un sensibile ecosistema con specie rari di animali come l'uccello frégate che è famoso per la sua apertura alare di due metri e secondo il quale l'isola porta il nome. In tempi passati l'isola serviva da nascondiglio per pirati e sembra che i pirati abbiano lasciato i loro tesori nei soggiorni e le camere da letto delle ville: letti intagliati a mano dall'Africa, sculture dal Java, cotone dall'Egitto.

Hidden inlets and tastefully designed suites — the daily routine seems light-years away.

Versteckte Buchten und geschmackvoll gestaltete Suiten — der Alltag scheint hier Lichtjahre entfernt.

Des baies cachées et des suites aménagées avec goût — le quotidien semble être à des années lumière.

Bahías escondidas y suites decoradas con gusto —la vida cotidiana parece estar a años luz de aquí.

Baie nascoste e suites create con gusto — la vita quotidiano sembra lontana anni di luce.

Pure relaxation: *sunbaths, plunging in the private whirlpool, or spending the day dreaming under the mosquito net in the picturesque villas.*

Erholung pur: *Sonnenbaden, in den privaten Whirlpool tauchen oder den Tag unter dem Moskitonetz in den pittoresken Villen verträumen.*

La détente pure : *prendre des bains de soleil, se baigner dans le jacuzzi privé ou passer la journée à rêver sous la moustiquaire des pittoresques villas.*

Descanso puro: *Tomar el sol, sumergirse en el jacuzzi privado o pasar el día en los pintorescos chalés soñando bajo el mosquitero.*

Rilassamento puro: *prendere il sole, immergersi nella vasca ad idromassaggio oppure sognare di giorno sotto la zanzariera nelle pittoresche ville.*

Lémuria Resort of Praslin

Praslin, Seychelles

Fans swirl warm tropical air through the thatch-roofed bungalows. Embedded in a coconut palm grove, they lie in the paradisiacal Bay of Kerlan with a spectacular sea view. To spare the island's flora and fauna, the bungalows were built purely out of natural materials such as teakwood, pink granite, and bamboo, since on the island, environmental protection comes first. Even the lighting was installed so that the turtles, laying eggs on the beach at night, remain undisturbed.

Ventilatoren wirbeln warme Tropenluft durch die strohgedeckten Bungalows. Eingebettet in einen Kokospalmenhain liegen sie in der paradiesischen Bucht von Kerlan mit spektakulärem Meerblick. Um Flora und Fauna der Insel zu schonen, wurden die Bungalows nur aus natürlichen Materialien wie Teakholz, rosafarbenem Granit und Bambus errichtet. Denn der Naturschutz steht auf den Inseln an erster Stelle. Sogar die Beleuchtung wurde so installiert, dass die Schildkröten, die nachts am Strand ihre Eier ablegen, ungestört bleiben.

Les ventilateurs font virevolter l'air chaud des tropiques dans les bungalows aux toits de paille. Implantées dans un bosquet de cocotiers, elles se trouvent dans la baie paradisiaque de Kerlan et jouissent d'une vue spectaculaire sur la mer. Afin de préserver la flore et la faune de l'île, les bungalows furent exclusivement construits à partir de matériaux naturels tels que le bois de teck, le granit rose et le bambous. En effet, la lutte pour la préservation de l'environnement est une priorité sur l'île. Même l'éclairage a été conçu de façon à ne pas déranger les tortues qui pondent des oeufs sur la plage la nuit venue.

Los ventiladores agitan el cálido aire tropical en los bungalows cubiertos de paja. Éstos están situados en la paradisíaca bahía Kerlan, rodeados por un bosque de palmas de coco, con una espectacular vista al mar. A fin de proteger la flora y fauna de la isla, los bungalows fueron construidos sólo con materiales naturales, como madera de teca, granito rosa y bambú, ya que la protección de los recursos naturales tiene prioridad absoluta en la isla. Incluso la iluminación fue instalada de tal forma que no perturbe a las tortugas que ponen sus huevos por la noche en la playa.

I ventilatori fanno girare l'aria tiepida tropicale nei bungalow ricoperti di paglia. Inseriti in un bosco d'alberi di noci di cocco si trovano nella paradisica baia di Kerlan, con una spettacolare vista sul mare. Per non disturbare la flora e fauna dell'isola, i bungalows sono stati eretti con soli materiali naturali come il legno teak, granito di color rosa e bambù. Infatti, il rispetto dell'ambiente tiene il primo posto sull'isola. Addirittura l'illuminazione è stata creata in modo da non disturbare le tartarughe che di notte depongono le loro uova sulla spiaggia.

The bungalows and terraces were harmoniously integrated into the tropical vegetation. Treating nature cautiously played an important role.

Harmonisch wurden Bungalows und Terrassen in die tropische Vegetation integriert. Dabei spielte der behutsame Umgang mit der Natur die wichtigste Rolle.

Les bungalows et les terrasses furent intégrés harmonieusement à la végétation tropicale. Le respect de la nature joue un rôle central.

Los bungalows y terrazas fueron integrados de manera armoniosa a la vegetación tropical, siendo lo más importante el manejo cuidadoso de las reservas naturales.

I bungalows e le terrazze sono state integrate armoniosamente nella vegetazione tropicale ove il rispetto per la natura gioca il ruolo più importante.

The lounge with a genuine sea of pillows on the veranda is an ideal hideaway for those seeking recuperation. Furniture in warm wood hues calms the senses.

Ideales Versteck für Erholungssuchende ist die Lounge mit einem wahren Meer aus Kissen auf der Veranda. Möbel in warmen Holztönen beruhigen die Sinne.

Les salons sont une cachette idéale pour ceux qui sont à la recherche de détente. Sous la véranda vous attendent une véritable mer de coussins. Les meubles construits en tons chauds de bois apaisent les sens.

Un escondite ideal para aquellos que buscan descansar es el salón con un verdadero mar de cojines en el porche.

La lounge con una marea di cuscini sulla veranda è il nascondiglio perfetto per chi cerca il relax. Mobili dalle calde tonalità del legno calmano i sensi.

North Island

North Island, Seychelles

4° 22' south, 55° 13' east—a position fixing to be noted. Because, the resort on this small island lets memories of heavenly circumstances arise. Hidden in the green of the trees, each of the eleven villas takes up 450 m². There, every conceivable comfort with an own refreshing pool, designer furniture, and a lawn in front of the terrace await. Yet, the lodge presents itself as environmentally sound and original: the style is half African, half Balinese.

4° 22' Süd, 55° 13' Ost – eine Positionsbestimmung zum Vormerken. Denn das Resort dieses kleinen Eilandes lässt Erinnerungen an paradiesische Zustände aufkommen. Versteckt im Grün der Bäume, misst jede der elf Villen 450 m². Darin wartet jeglicher Komfort mit eigenem Erfrischungspool, Designermöbeln und Liegewiese vor der Terrasse. Gleichwohl präsentiert sich die Lodge umweltschonend und ursprünglich: im Stil halb afrikanisch, halb balinesisch.

4° 22' Sud, 55° 13' Est – une position dont on doit se souvenir. En effet, le domaine de cette petite île réveille des souvenirs d'état paradisiaque. Cachées dans le vert des arbres, chacune des onze villas mesurent 450 m². Là, vous attend un confort complet et une piscine privée pour vous rafraîchir, des meubles de designers et un gazon de détente devant la terrasse. Le pavillon a une apparence naturelle et originelle : de style moitié africain, moitié balinais.

4° 22' Sur, 55° 13' Este –una posición para tomar en cuenta, ya que el resort en esta pequeña isla evoca sensaciones paradisíacas. Escondidos tras el verde de los árboles, cada uno de los once villas tiene 450 m². Aquí se encuentran todo tipo de comodidades: Una piscina propia, muebles de diseño y un prado para recostarse delante de la terraza. No obstante, el diseño es auténtico y compatible con el medio ambiente: Un estilo mitad africano, mitad balinés.

4° 22' Sud, 55° 13' Est – una posizione da ricordarsi, perchè il resort di questa piccola isola fa venire in mente il ricordo del paradiso. Nascoste nel verde degli alberi, ognuna delle undici ville misura 450 m². Al loro interno si trova ogni genere di confort con la propria piscina per rinfrescarsi, mobili fatti da designers e il prato per sdaiarsi davanti alla terrazza. Allo stesso tempo il lodge si presenta in modo rispettoso per l'ambiente ed originale: uno stile misto tra l'africano ed il balinese.

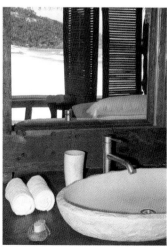

Living like Robinson Crusoe without having to relinquish on western luxury—that is the special charm of North Island.

Leben wie Robinson Crusoe ohne auf westlichen Luxus verzichten zu müssen – darin liegt der besondere Reiz von North Island.

Vivre comme Robinson Crusoé, sans renoncer cependant au luxe occidental – c'est le défit relevé par North Island.

Vivir como Robinson Crusoe sin tener que renunciar al lujo occidental –eso es lo que hace especialmente atractiva la North Island.

Vivere come Robinson Crusoe senza dover rinunciare al lusso dell'Ovest - è questo il particolare fascino della North Island.

In the Piazza lounge, the main building on North Island, one often meets distinguished guests in the evenings. In comparison, the romantic tasteful rooms in the huts are more intimate.

In der Lounge der Piazza, dem Haupthaus auf North Island, trifft sich abends oft eine illustre Gesellschaft. Intimer sind dagegen die romantisch-stilvollen Plätze in den Hütten.

Dans le salon de la piazza, la maison centrale de North Island, une société illustre se retrouve parfois le soir. Plus intimes sont les places romantiques et plein de style situées dans les cabanes.

En el lounge de la Piazza, la casa principal de North Island, se reúnen por las noches, con frecuencia, los famosos de la sociedad. Son más intimos, en cambio, los lugares románticos y elegantes en las cabañas.

Nella lounge della Piazza, l'edificio principale del North Island, di sera ci s'incontra una comunità variopinta. Sono invece più intimi i posti romantici e di stile nelle capanne.

The resort contributes to the preservation of a unique natural environment—and offers the greatest possible seclusion at the same time.

Das Resort trägt zum Erhalt einer einzigartigen Natur bei — und bietet gleichzeitig eine größtmögliche Abgeschiedenheit.

Le domaine participe à la préservation de la nature exceptionnelle qui l'entoure — et offre un isolement total.

El resort contribuye a la conservación de una naturaleza única y, al mismo tiempo, permite un gran recogimiento.

Il resort contribuisce alla conservazione di una natura unica — ed offre allo stesso tempo il massimo della solitudine.

North Island *North Island, Seychelles*   213

Alfajiri Villas

Diani Beach, Kenya

Having set foot on the soft sand on Kenya's south coast, one returns over and again. On Diani Beach, the Italian owners of Alfajiri have secured one of the loveliest spots. Lamu carved doors and African and Far East art adorn the Cliff, Garden and Beach Villa with their high Makuti roofs. With mosquito nets over the beds, one sleeps with the window open and listens to the waves. Daytime, shady arbors invite one to dream. Beach fans find an exclusive, tasteful sanctuary here.

Wer einmal den Puderzucker-Sand an der Südküste Kenias betreten hat, kommt immer wieder. Einen der schönsten Plätze am Diani Beach haben sich die italienischen Inhaber von Alfajiri gesichert. Geschnitzte Türen aus Lamu und Kunst aus Afrika und Fernost zieren die Cliff-, Garden- und Beach Villa mit ihren hohen Makuti-Dächern. Mit Moskitonetzen über den Betten schläft man bei offenem Fenster und hört den Wellen zu. Tagsüber laden schattige Lauben zum Träumen ein. Strandfans finden hier ein exklusives, stilvolles Refugium.

Celui qui aura déjà marché sur le sable fin comme le sucre en poudre des côtes méridionales du Kenya, reviendra toujours. Les propriétaires italiens de Alfajiri possèdent une des plus belles places de la Diani Beach. Des portes en lamu sculptées, de l'art originaire d'Afrique et d'Extrême-Orient décorent les villas situées sur la falaise, dans les jardins et en bord de mer qui arborent leurs hauts toits de makuti. On dort avec des moustiquaires, la fenêtre ouverte en écoutant les vagues. La journée, les tonnelles ombrageuses invitent à la rêverie. Les fans de la plage trouvent ici un refuge exclusif et plein de style.

Quien haya pisado alguna vez la arena tan fina como azúcar en polvo de la costa del sur de Kenia, vuelve una y otra vez. Los propietarios de Alfajiri, de nacionalidad italiana, se aseguraron uno de los sitios más hermosos en la playa Diani. Puertas de Lamu talladas y piezas de arte de África y del Extremo Oriente adornan los chalés Cliff, Garden y Beach, con sus altos techos de makuti. Con mosquiteros sobre las camas es posible dormir con las ventanas abiertas y escuchar el ruido de las olas. De día, el ramaje umbrío invita a soñar. Los fanáticos de la playa encuentran aquí un refugio exclusivo y de gran estilo.

Chi ha messo piede per la prima volta sulla spiaggia a zucchero di velo della costa meridionale del Kenia, ritornerà sempre di nuovo. I proprietari italiani dell'Alfajiri si sono assicurati uno dei posti più belli della Diani Beach. Porte intagliate di lamu ed arte dall'Africa e l'Estremo Oriente decorano le Cliff-, Garden e Beach Villa con i loro alti tetti di makuti. Con le zanzariere sopra i letti ci si dorme con finestre aperte, ascoltando le onde. Di giorno padiglioni ombreggiati nel giardino invitano a sognare. I fans della spiaggia qui trovano un rifugio esclusivo e di stile.

Living with farsightedness: *Over three floors, the villa rises over the pool and the turquoise colored Indian Ocean.*

Wohnen mit Weitblick: *Über drei Etagen erhebt sich die Villa über den Pool und den türkisfarbenen Indischen Ozean.*

Vivre le regard *perdu dans l'horizon : la villa s'élève sur trois étages au-dessus de la piscine et de l'océan Indien turquoise.*

Disfrutar de *una amplia vista: Con más de tres pisos se yergue la edificación sobre la piscina y las aguas de color turquesa del Océano Índico.*

Abitare con *un'ampia vista: la villa si estende su tre piani sopra la piscina e l'Oceano Indiano di colore turchese.*

Index

California

San Diego

Hotel del Coronado

1500 Orange Avenue, Coronado, California 92118, USA
T +1 (619) 435 6611   F +1 (619) 522 8262
www.hoteldel.com

688 rooms, suites and cottages located in a 31 acres terrain at the Pacific Ocean. Four Restaurants: Sheerwater Restaurant (coastal dining), Prince of Wales (classical fine cuisine), Babcock & Story Bar (cocktailbar) and Crown Room (events and Sunday brunch). 2 swimming pools, Spa and fitness center. 15 minutes to San Diego International Airport.

Los Angeles

Shutters on the Beach

1 Pico Blvd., Santa Monica, California 90405, USA
T +1 (310) 458 0030, F +1 (310) 458 4589
www.shuttersonthebeach.com

186 rooms and 12 suites in 3 separate buildings. 3 Presidential Suites with whirlpool, bathtub and fire place. 2 restaurants. Pool and sun deck. Spa, health club. Ballroom, 3 meeting rooms. Situated near the historic pier, 8 miles from Los Angeles International Airport.

Dana Point

St. Regis Monarch Beach Resort & Spa

1 Monarch Beach Resort, Dana Point, California 92629, USA
T +1 (949) 234 3200, F +1 (949) 234 3201
www.stregismb.com

326 rooms, 74 suites including 2 Presidential Suites with balcony, piano and fireplace. Ocean-view dining at each of the 8 restaurants and lounges. Aqua seafood restaurant (chef: Bruno Chemel). 2 Ballrooms, 6 meeting rooms. Spa. 18-hole golf course, tennis club with 6 hard and 2 lighted clay courts. Kid's Club. 1 hour from Los Angeles International Airport.

Florida

Miami

Mandarin Oriental Miami

500 Brickell Key Drive, Miami, Florida 33131, USA
T +1 (305) 913 8288, F +1 (305) 9138300
www.mandarinoriental.com

327 rooms, 31 suites with balconies. Mandarin Suite with own private spa sanctuary. Azul gourmet restaurant (chef: Michelle Bernstein), restaurant, lobby lounge, bar. Ballroom up to 600 people, 15 meeting rooms, business center. Spa with 17 treatment rooms. Located 20 minutes from Miami International Airport.

Miami

The Ritz-Carlton, South Beach

1 Lincoln Road, Miami Beach, Florida 33139, USA
T +1 (786) 276 4000, F +1 (786) 476 4100
www.ritzcarlton

376 guest rooms and suites. Original art collection featuring established and emerging artists. 3 restaurants, beach club, Lapidus Lounge featuring lounge music created especially for the hotel. Spa with 14 treatment rooms. Conference facilities. Children's program The Ritz Kids. Located directly on Miami Beach, 20 minutes from Miami International Airport.

Palm Beach

The Breakers

1 South County Road, Palm Beach, Florida 33480, USA
T +1 (561) 655 6611, F +1 (561) 659 8403
www.thebreakers.com

560 guest rooms, 57 suites including 2 Imperial Suites and 2 Royal Poinciana Suites. 5 restaurants, 3 bars. Spa. Children's programmes. Conference facilities. Two 18-hole championship golf courses, tennis. Located 7 miles from Palm Beach International Airport.

Bahamas

Paradise Island

One&Only Ocean Club

Paradise Island, Bahamas
T +1 (242) 363 2501, F +1 (242) 363 2424
www.oneandonlyresorts.com

106 rooms including 14 suites nestled in 2 wings of different small buildings, garden cottages and villas. 2 restaurants, pool terrace café, gourmet in-room dining. Full-service Spa, 2 pools. 18-hole championship golf course, 6 tennis courts, complimentary non-motorized water sports. 2 meeting rooms for small meetings. Located a short ride from Nassau International Airport.

Great Exuma

Four Seasons Resort Great Exuma at Emerald Bay

P.O. Box EX 29005, Great Exuma, Bahamas
T +1 (242) 336 6800   F +1 (242) 336 6801
www.fourseasons.com

183 guest rooms and suites with terrace or balcony, 2 Royal Beachfront Villas each with private pool. Restaurant, grill and lounge. Full-service Spa, Spa garden, health club, steam, massage. 18-hole championship golf course, 6 tennis courts, watersports. Supervised activities for children and children's pool. 15 minutes from Exuma International Airport.

Mexico

Puerto Vallarta

Las Alamandas

Km. 83,5 Carretera Barra de Navidad, Puerto Vallarta, Quémaro, Jalisco, Mexico 48980
T +52 (322) 285 5500, F +52 (322) 285 5027
www.lasalamandas.com
www.mexicoboutiquehotels.com/lasalamandas

6 villas with 14 suites for maximum 28 guests, villas with indoor/outdoor lounge areas, high-pitched tile roofs, private terraces and full-sized living/dining areas. Beach club, restaurant and bar. Conference room. Fitness center, tennis court, swimming pool Golf nearby. Private asphalt runway for small aircrafts, 1 ½ hours drive from Manzanillo Airport.

Punta Mita

Four Seasons Resort Punta Mita

Punta Mita, Bahia de Banderas, Nayarit, Mexico 63734
T +52 (329) 291 6000, F +52 (329) 291 6021
www.fourseasons.com

140 rooms including 26 suites, all suites include either a private plunge pool or terrace. 3 restaurants with shaded garden terraces and ocean view, pool bar and lounge. Spa, infinity pool, fitness center, water sports, 4 tennis courts, 8-hole golf course. Children's programs. 40 minutes from Puerto Vallarta International Airport.

Costalegre

El Tamarindo

Km 7,5 Carretera Melaque to Puerto Vallarta
Cihuatlán, Jalisco, Mexico 48970
T +52 (315) 351 5032, F +52 (315) 351 5070
www.mexicoboutiquehotels.com

29 villas with private plunge pool, nestled in a 2,040-acre ecological reserve. Restaurant, bar, lounge. 3 private beaches and private pier. 18-hole championship golf course on the property, tennis courts. Pool, jungle Spa. 3.5 hours south of Puerto Vallarta and 50 minutes north of Manzanillo Airport.

Riviera Maya

Ikal del Mar

Playa Xcalacoco, Riviera Maya, Quintana Roo, Mexico 77710
T +52 (984) 877 3000, F +52 (984) 877 3009
www.ikaldelmar.com

29 villas with private pool and 1 presidential villa. Restaurant, bar. Swimming pool, full service Spa with Temazcal bath (traditional Mayan bath ritual), beauty salon. At night the property is illuminated with torches and no motorized vehicles are allowed. 40 miles drive from Cancun International Airport.

Los Cabos

One&Only Palmilla

Km 7,5 Carretera Transpeninsular, San José Del Cabo, BCS, Mexico CP 23400
T +52 (624) 146 7000, F +52 (624) 146 7001
www.oneandonlyresorts.com

173 rooms and suites with patio or balcony. Personal butler service. C seafood restaurant and restaurant with Mexiterranean cuisine, outdoor bar and lounge. Spa, fitness center. Conference center, ballroom. 18-hole Jack Nicklaus championship golf course. Watersports and whale watching. 20 minutes from José del Cabo International Airport.

Los Cabos

Las Ventanas al Paraiso

Km 19,5 Carretera Transpeninsular, San José del Cabo, Baja California Sur. Mexico 23400
T +52 (624) 144 2800, F +52 (624) 144 2801
www.lasventanas.com

61 suites including a 3,000-square-feet 3-bedroom suite with private pool and rooftop terrace, all suites with fireplaces. 2 restaurants with open-air and air-conditioned areas, grill, wine room and bar. Spa, sauna, steam and whirlpool, beach pavilion for massage therapies. 2 tennis courts, watersports including snorkeling, scubadiving, windsurfing, sea kayaking, sport fishing. 20 minutes from San José del Cabo International Airport.

France

Cap Ferrat

Grand Hôtel du Cap-Ferrat

71 boulevard Général de Gaulle, 06230 Saint-Jean-Cap-Ferrat, France
T +33 (4) 93 76 5050, F +33 (4) 93 76 0452
www.grand-hotel-cap-ferrat.com

44 rooms, 9 suites and Villa Rose-Pierre. Gourmet restaurant Le Cap, poolside Club Dauphin with view over the Mediterranean Sea. Conference rooms with natural daylight and view on the pine gardens. Situated between Nice and Monaco surrounded by a private parc, 20 km from Nice International Airport.

Greece

Chalkidiki

Danai Beach Resort

Nikiti, Sithonia, 63088 Chalkidiki, Greece
T +30 (237) 50 22310, F +30 (237) 50 22591
www.dbr.gr

61 rooms, suites and villas. 18 of the suites with private pool, most of the rooms have hydro-massage. 3 restaurants including gourmet restaurant, bar. The resort hosts celebrity guest chefs from 1- and 2-star Michelin restaurants. Spa, steam bath, saunas, jacuzzi. 50 minutes drive from Makedonia International Airport Thessaloniki.

Crete

Blue Palace Resort & Spa

P.O. Box 38 Elounda, 72053 Island of Crete, Greece
T +30 (28410) 65500, F +30 (28410) 89712
www.bluepalace.gr

106 units of bungalows, suites and 3 villas, some with private pools. 5 restaurants including gourmet venue, 2 bars and lounge with sea view. Spa offering a complete range of wet and dry Thalasso treatments, steam baths, saunas, jacuzzis indoor and outdoor, heated pool, gym. Conference facilities for up to 230 people. 1 hour drive from Heraklion Airport.

India

Goa

Park Hyatt Goa Resort & Spa

Arrossim Beach, Cansaulim, South Goa 403 712, India
T +91 (832) 272 1234, F +91 (832) 272 1235
www.goa.regency.hyatt.com

251 rooms with verandas or balconies, some with outdoor shower. 4 Restaurants offering Goan specialities, seafood, Italian and vegetarian cuisine. 2 bars. Ballroom and 2 function rooms. Spa with Ayurvedic treatments and new-age therapies. Land and water sports. 15 minutes from Goa International Airport.

Goa

The Leela Goa

Mobor, Goa 403 731, India
T +91 (832) 2871234, F +91 (832) 2871352
www.theleela.com

137 rooms and suites with either balcony or private patio, The Royal Villa and Presidential Villa have own plunge pools. 3 restaurants offering Indian, Italian, Asian and European cuisine. Beach side barbecue and grill restaurant, 3 bars, 1 with discotheque. Ballroom and conference rooms. 47 km from Goa International Airport.

Maldives

Kuda Huraa

Four Seasons Resort Maldives at Kuda Huraa

North Malé Atoll, Maldives
T +960 444 888, F +960 441 188
www.fourseasons.com

106 bungalows and villas including 38 water bungalows and 26 beach bungalows with private plunge pools. 3 restaurants, lounge, poolside terrace and bar. Spa on private island, lagoon-side fitness center. Cruises aboard the Four Seasons Explorer, PADI dive center, water sports center. 25 minutes from Malé International Airport by speedboat.

Makunufushi

Cocoa Island

Makunufushi, South Malé Atoll, Maldives
T +960 441818, F +960 441919
www.cocoa-island.com

Private island resort with 17 suites and 4 villas with private sun decks. Sunset villa with private jetty. Restaurant and bar, Como Shambhala cuisine. Swimming pool, Como Shambhala retreat offering a full range of treatments. Fully equipped dive center, watersports. Situated 30 minutes by speedboat from Malé International Airport.

Malé Atoll

Taj Exotica Resort & Spa

Emboodhu Finolhu, South Malé Atoll, Maldives
T +960 442200, F +960 442211
www.tajhotels.com

64 villas including 4 Deluxe Beach Villas with plunge pools and the Rehendhi Suite. 2 restaurants and bar, 24 hours in-villa dining. Spa with outdoor massage pavilion. Fitness center, freshwater swimming pool, PADI diving and water sports center. 15 minutes by speedboat from Malé International Airport.

Rangali Island

Hilton Maldives

Rangali Island, P.O. Box 2034, Rangali Island, NA MV 2034 Maldives
T +960 4 50629, F +960 4 50619
www.maldives.hilton.com

25 Beach Villas, 75 Deluxe Beach Villas and 40 Water Villas. 3 restaurants and 2 bars, sand-floored buffet restaurant, wine cellar, grill and bar set atop a coral reef. Spa, fitness room, pool. Scuba diving, water sports center, tennis court. The resort is built on 2 islands, linked by a footbridge. 30 minutes from Malé International Airport by seaplane.

Indonesia

Bali

Amankila

Manggis, Bali, Indonesia
T +62 (363) 41333, F +62 (363) 41555
www.amanresorts.com

34 free-standing suites, some with private pools, Amankila Suite with 2 separate pavilions, private pool, and private butler service. 2 restaurants and beach club. Private dining available in the suites 24 hours. 3 pools, traditional Balinese massage and beauty treatments available in the guest suites, in the massage pavilion or at the Beach Club. 1 hour from Bali International Airport.

Bali

Four Seasons Resort Bali at Jimbaran Bay

Jimbaran, Denpasar, Bali, Indonesia 80361
T +62 (361) 701010, F +62 (361) 701020
www.fourseasons.com

147 villas with plunge pool. 4 restaurants and 2 bars including Indonesian and Western cuisine, exotic Asian noodle dishes and beachfront dining. Full service Spa and wellness facilities offering traditional Indonesian beauty and massage treatments. Cooking school. Complimentary water sports. 15 minutes from Ngurah Rai International Airport.

Bali

The Legian & Club at The Legian

Jalan Laksmana, Seminyak Beach, Bali 80361
T +62 (361) 730 622, F +62 (361) 730 623
www.ghmhotels.com

67 suites, 14 with two bedrooms and an area of 150 m², 10 villas in the Club at The Legian. Bar and brasserie style restaurant with traditional Indonesian and other Asian food. Meeting facilities for 50 persons. Library and CD-collection. Spa with sauna and massage facilities.

Thailand

Phuket

Amanpuri

Pansea Beach, Phuket 83000, Thailand
T +66 (76) 324 333 , F +66 (76) 324 100
www.amanresorts.com

40 pavilions with private outdoor terrace, 30 Thai villas with private pool. 2 restaurants, pool bar. 24 hours room service. Spa, meditation and yoga sessions, swimming pool, gym, library, tailor services. Snorkeling equipment and water-skiing, selection of boats for cruises and excursions. 25 km drive to Phuket Airport.

Phuket

Banyan Tree Phuket

33 Moo 4, Srisoonthorn Rd.
Cherngtalay Amphur Talang, Phuket 83110, Thailand
T +66 (76) 324 374, F +66 (76) 324 375
www.banyantree.com

123 villas with own garden, 55 of them with private swimming pool, some villas with outdoor jacuzzi and shower, open-air sunken bath tub, in-villa Spa. 4 restaurants. Spa, yoga. 18-hole golf course, tenniscourts, sailing and windsurfing. 1 hour and 15 minutes flight from Bangkok.

Phuket

JW Marriott Phuket Resort and Spa

1 Moo 3, Mai Khao, Talang Phuket 83116, Thailand
T +66 (76) 330 000, F +66 (76) 348 348
www.marriott.com

265 Rooms on 3 floors. 4 restaurants. Health club with whirlpool, sauna and Spa facilities, some treatment rooms with a plunge pool and garden shower. 10 meeting rooms and ballroom for up to 450 people. Children's programs at The Little Turtle's Club. 2 outdoor swimming pools and children's pool, tennis courts, golf course nearby. 15 minutes from Phuket International Airport.

Pranburi

Aleenta

Pran Buri, Phuket, Thailand
T +66 (2) 519 2044, F +66 (2) 519 2045
www.aleenta.com

3 Pool Suites with private plunge pools, 2 Beach Houses with private plunge pool or rooftop deck, 4 Ocean View Suites with sunken stone tubs, 1 Penthouse with sunken stone tub, 3 Grand Villas with patio and sun deck opened to the sea. Restaurant, bar and pool lounge. Private dining available. Spa with outdoor Spa. 45 minutes from Hua Hin Airport.

Vietnam

Nha Trang

Ana Mandara Resort

Beachside Tran Phu Blvd, Nha Trang, Vietnam
T +84 (58) 829 829, F +84 (58) 829 629
www.sixsenses.com

17 villas containing 68 guest rooms with private terrace. 2 restaurants and bars. Spa with outdoor treatment salas, jacuzzi baths, Vichy shower and Japanese style bath, saunas and steams. Water sports on resort's private beach. 40 minutes from Cam Ranh Airport.

Australia

th Queensland

Bedarra Island

Bedarra Island, Great Barrier Reef, Australia
T +61 (7) 4068 8233, F +61 (7) 4068 8215
www.bedarraisland.com

16 rooms with private balcony, pavilions and villas, some with private plunge pool. Restaurant, bar and lounge. Gourmet picnics available. Massages. 18-hole golf course on neighboring Dunk Island. Scuba diving trips to Great Barrier Reef, watersports and tennis. Flights via Cairns and Dunk Island, boat transfer from Dunk Island 15 minutes, helicopter flights available.

Fiji Islands

Vatulele Island

Vatulele Island Resort

Vatulele, Fiji Islands
T +61 (2) 9665 8700, F +61 (2) 9665 7833 (Sydney office only)
www.vatulele.com

18 villas, The Point Villa with air-conditioning and a pool-fresh water. Communal dining room for all clients, private dining available either in own room, on the beach, in the wine cellar, in a Gazebo overlooking the beach. Massage available. Helipad. 25 minutes by light aircraft from Nadi International Airport.

French Polynesia

Bora Bora

Bora Bora Nui Resort & Spa

Motu Toopua, Nunue, Bora Bora, French Polynesia
T +689 603 300, F +689 603 301
www.starwood.com/luxury

120 luxury suites and bungalows, including over water bungalows, beach bungalows and hillside bungalows. Panoramic restaurant, poolside grill and 2 bars, 1 with lagoon view. Outdoor pool. 6 miles from Motu Mute Domestic Airport.

United Arab Emirates

Dubai

Beit al Bahar Villa

P.O. Box 11416, Dubai, U.A.E.
T +971 (4) 348 0000, F +971 (4) 348 2273
www.jumeirahinternational.com

19 villas with terrace, plunge pool and personal service. 2 restaurants. Private dining in the villas available. Children's Club Sinbad's and 4 pools situated at the Jumeirah Beach Hotel. Watersports, 3 squash courts, gym, yoga and karate. 7 floodlit tennis courts. Health suite. 3 golf courses within 20 km. 30 minutes from Dubai International Airport.

Dubai

One&Only Royal Mirage

P.O. Box 37252, Dubai, U.A.E.
T +971 (4) 399 99 99, F +971 (4) 399 99 9
www.oneandonlyresorts.com

The resort comprises 3 properties: The Palace, the Arabian Court and the Residence & Spa. The Palace has 226 rooms and 20 suites with private balcony or terrace. The Arabian court has 162 rooms and 10 suites with private balcony or terrace. The Residence has 3 Royal Villas, 18 suites and 32 deluxe rooms. 7 restaurants, beach bar, grill, rooftop bar, lounge. Health club, Spa, hammam. 20 minutes from Dubai International Airport.

Egypt

Sharm El Sheikh

Four Seasons Resort Sharm El Sheikh

1 Four Seasons Boulevard, P.O. Box 203, Sharm El Sheikh, Sinai Peninsula
T +20 (69) 603 555, F +20 (69) 603 550
www.fourseasons.com

136 rooms including 27 suites with balcony or terrace, 12 with private plunge pools. 3 restaurants, grill and pool bar, 2 lounges. Beauty and wellness Spa, pool, outdoor massage areas. Children's pool. 4 tennis courts, 2 of them floodlit. Coral reef snorkelling and scuba diving, water sports. 10 minutes from Sharm El Sheikh International Airport.

Oman

Muscat

The Chedi Muscat

North Ghubra 232, Way No. 3215, Street No. 46,
Muscat, Sultanate of Oman
T +968 50 44 00, F +968 24 49 34 85
www.ghmhotels.com

61 Superior Rooms, 60 Deluxe Rooms, 40 Chedi Club Suites. Restaurant offering contemporary Mediterranean and Asian cuisine, lobby lounge and 2 poolside cabanas. Spa, fitness center. Tennis courts. 2 swimming pools (1 for adults over 16 years, 1 for families). 20 minutes from Muscat airport.

Mauritius

Poste de Flacq

Le Prince Maurice

Choisy Road, Poste de Flacq, Maurice
T +230 413 9100, F +230 413 9130
www.constancehotels.com

89 suites, including 12 Senior Suites with swimming pool and Princely Suite on the beach with garden/patio, 3 terraces and 2 swimming pools. 2 restaurants, 2 bars. Two 18-hole championship golf courses. Health center, Guerlain Institute, massages. Air conditioned squash court, gym, jacuzzi, sauna, aerobics and yoga. 45 km from the airport.

Belle Mare

The Residence

Coastal Road, Belle Mare, Maurice
T +230 401 88 88, F +230 415 58 88
www.theresidence.com

135 rooms and 28 suites. The Dining Room restaurant and The Verandah offer á la carte dining, Western cuisine and local specialities. The Plantation restaurant offers Creole and seafood cuisine, lounge bar. Sanctuary Spa, massage. Watersports, 3 tennis courts. Childrens' club. 50 minutes from the airport.

Trou d'Eau Douce

One&Only Le Touessrok

Trou d'Eau Douce, Maurice
T +230 402 7400, F +230 402 7500
www.oneandonlyresorts.com

37 Deluxe rooms, 32 Junior Suites and Royal Suite on the mainland. Coral Wing with 31 Deluxe rooms and 1 Junior Suite. 98 suites on private Frangipani Island —linked to the mainland by a wooden bridge. 6 restaurants and bars. 18-hole golf course nearby. Children's club with tree house, pool and computer room. Located on the east coast, 50 minutes from the airport.

Seychelles

Mahé Island

Banyan Tree Seychelles

Anse Intendance, Mahé, Seychelles
T +248 383 500, F +248 383 600
ww.banyantree.com/seychelles

36 pool villas with verandas, jacuzzi and swimming pools. Presidential Villa with infinity pool, outdoor Jacuzzi and large sundeck and living pavilion. 5 restaurants, pool bar. Spa. Infinity pool, Island hopping excursions and water sport facilities. Located 30 minutes by car from Mahé International Airport.

Frégate Island

Frégate Island Private

Frégate Island, Seychelles
T +49 (6102) 501 321, F +49 (6102) 501 322 (Unique Experiences)
www.fregate.com

16 villas with terraces and jacuzzi, 14 on top of the cliffs with panoramic views, 2 of them nestled in private gardens. Private Island limited to max. 40 guests. 2 restaurants, bar, private beach, pool, gym, health club. Castaway Kid's Club, babysitting service. PADI dive center, Hobie Cat sailing, guided hikes through the island's jungle. Golf course nearby on Praslin Island. 20 minutes from Mahé by private aircraft.

Praslin

Lémuria Resort of Praslin

Anse Kerlan, Praslin, Seychelles
T +248 281 281, F +248 281 000
www.lemuriaresort.com

80 junior suites, 8 senior suites, each positioned 15 meters from the shore, nestled in a natural botanical garden. 3 restaurants offering Sechellois and French cuisine, 4 bars, sauna, jacuzzi. Children's club. 2 tennis courts, golf course. Located on the northwest coast, 5 minutes away from Praslin airstrip.

North Island

North Island

North Island, Indian Ocean, Seychelles
T + 2 48 29 3100, F +2 48 29 3150
www.north-island.com

11 spacious villas with private lounge, plunge pool, kitchenette. Sliding doors allow uninterrupted views. Each villa is equipped with an electro-buggy and 2 bicycles. Cuisine with "no menu concept". Each menu created individually by the head chef. Sunset beach bar. Spa with outdoor area. 5 beaches including a private honeymoon beach. 15 minutes from Mahé by helicopter.

Kenya

Diani Beach

Alfajiri Villas

Diani Beach, Kenia
T +254 (040) 320 2630, F +254 (040) 320 2218
www.alfajirivillas.com

3 luxury villas for up to 8 guests with pools, verandas. Mediterranean light cuisine with fresh seafood. Massage and reflexology. Tennis, squash and a health club nearby. Windsurfing and snorkeling, diving courses, deep sea fishing. 18-hole championship golf course located nearby. Safaris. Located on the south coast of Mombasa, 5 minutes from Ukunda Airstrip and 1 hour from Mombasa Airport.

Photo Credits

Editor Martin Nicholas Kunz

Editorial coordination Patricia Massó

Introduction Christian Schönwetter

Hotel texts by Bärbel Holzberg, Heinfried Tacke, Camilla Péus, Christian Schönwetter, Martin Nicholas Kunz

Layout & Prepress Käthe Nennstiel

Imaging Susanne Olbrich

Translations
English AdeTeam, Robert Kaplan
French Kern AG Sprachendienste
Spanish Christina Franco
Italian Jaqueline Rizzo

Editorial project by fusion publishing gmbh, Berlin.
www.fusion-publishing.com

Published by teNeues Publishing Group

teNeues Verlag GmbH + Co. KG
Am Selder 37, 47906 Kempen, Germany
Tel.: 0049-(0)2152-916-0, Fax: 0049-(0)2152-916-111
Press department: arehn@teneues.de

teNeues Publishing Company
16 West 22nd Street, New York, NY 10010, USA
Tel.: 001-212-627-9090, Fax: 001-212-627-9511

teNeues Publishing UK Ltd.
York Villa, York Road, Byfleet, KT14 7HX, Great Britain
Tel.: 0044-1932-403509, Fax: 0044-1932-403514

teNeues France S.A.R.L.
93, rue Bannier, 45000 Orléans, France
Tel.: 0033-2-38541071, Fax: 0033-2-38625340

www.teneues.com

© 2009 teNeues Verlag GmbH + Co. KG, Kempen

Anniversary Edition

ISBN: 978-3-8327-9334-0

Printed in Italy

Bibliographic information published by Die Deutsche Nationalbibliothek
The Deutsche Nationalbibliothek lists this publication in the Deutsche Nationalbibliografie; detailed bibliographic data are available in the Internet at http://dnb.d-nb.de